FATHER ALEXANDER MEN
MARTYR OF ATHEISM

MICHEL EVDOKIMOV

Translated by Margaret Parry

Foreword by Neville Kyrke-Smith

Introduction by Metropolitan Kallistos of Diokleia

GRACEWING

First published in French as
Petite vie du père Men
by
Desclée de Brouwer, Paris

First published in England in 2011
by
Gracewing
2 Southern Avenue
Leominster
Herefordshire HR6 0QF
United Kingdom
www.gracewing.co.uk

ISBN 978 085244 608 9

On the cover: photo of Fr Men in later life.

Typeset by Gracewing

CONTENTS

Contents..3

Foreword by Neville Kyrke-Smith............................5

Introduction by Metropolitan Kallistos of Diokleia...7

Preface 11

1. At that time a great persecution arose against the
Church 15

Spare your people, O Lord!...............................16
See how my enemies have humiliated me 25

2. The child grew and the Lord blessed him............29

Many shall rejoice at his birth............................29
Instruct the child in the way he should go....................31
Ezra had prepared his heart to seek the law of the Lord...35

3. The law shall not perish for want of priests.........41

He was called to enter the temple of the Lord...................43
The number of those who believed in the Lord increased...46
On each Sabbath all flesh shall come to worship before me..50

4. This is the Church of which I am made a minister
to you 57

So that you might be partakers of the divine nature....... 57
Narrow is the gate which leads to life...............................61

5. You renew the face of the earth............................69

Let us walk in newness of life.............................69

Their unbelief shall not cancel God's faithfulness............75

We are taken for dying, and behold, we live....................80

There must be divisions amongst you...............................86

6. He shall be saved as by fire.....................................93

Watch and pray, for you know neither the day nor the hour..93

Enter into the joy of your Lord..100

FOREWORD

Not long ago I was standing in the rain in the Russian woods in Semkhoz, a small village an hour and a half from Moscow. I had come to visit the place where Father Alexander Men was axed to death on Sunday 9 September 1990. Rain dripped from the silver birch trees to the mossy earth, like heavenly tears being shed for a modern martyr. As I prayed and meditated, I recalled my first visit to Fr Alexander's resting place, just after his brutal murder, how I had stood alongside his simple grave with his family. His murderers have never been found—although in the weeks before his death he described being followed and watched. Maybe he was killed because of his Jewish background? Or because he was socially active, challenging people to live a Christian life which would impact on society? Perhaps he was considered too large and influential a public figure because of his appearances on television, radio and in the papers?

Yet, Father Alexander's witness and his challenge to live a Christian life in the world are not forgotten. He still inspires those searching for a meaning to, and a path through, life. He desired to live, to speak, to transmit 'the authentic message of Christ' through a deep prayer life centred on the Liturgy and by personally engaging with those he met. His openness drew people to him. In an interview Fr Alexander said: 'Every religion is a path towards God, a conjecture about God, a human approach to God – a vector pointing upwards from below. But the coming of Christ is the answer, a vector coming from heaven towards us.'[1]

Fr Alexander had his own followers—perhaps we might even call them 'disciples of Men'—who have initiated important projects in his memory, many of which Aid to the Church in Need has been privileged to support. His witness lives on, spanning cultural and ecumenical divides. May we too find something in this moving and meditative tribute to inspire us to become 'disciples of Men' for the good of all Mankind. May he rest in peace.

Neville Kyrke-Smith
National Director
Aid to the Church in Need UK

---

[1] Transcript of interview with Mark Makarov, published 1992 and quoted in *Christianity for the Twenty-First Century: The Life and Work of Alexander Men*, edited by Elizabeth Roberts and Ann Shukman, SCM: 1996.

INTRODUCTION

F R ALEXANDER MEN (1935-90), as this concise but penetrating biography makes clear, was a highly effective parish priest, drawing worshippers from many miles around, whose sermons were followed with close and eager attention. More than that, in his Lectures and in his numerous books—often written in the night hours after a busy and exhausting day of pastoral work—he displayed an exceptional gift as a teacher and communicator, capable of reaching members of the intelligentsia alienated from the Church by atheist propaganda. But, above all, he possessed an unusually attractive personality: warm, lively, challenging, full of humour. I am indeed grateful to Fr Michel Evdokimov for recounting in such sympathetic terms the life of this extraordinary man, and to Margaret Parry for making this work available to English readers.

In an address given on 8 September 1990, on the night before he was murdered, Fr Alexander said characteristically, 'The history of Christianity has only just begun.' He was supremely a man of hope, open to the future, who considered that we are living at the beginning of a new era. Yet at other moments he wondered whether we might not be at the end rather than the beginning. 'Our century may be the last in history,' he suggested. 'Perhaps we have reached the end of civilization.' This gave to all that he did and said a sense of urgency and crisis. He emphasized the need to live wholeheartedly in the present moment: 'When you work, work. When you pray, pray. When you play, play. Do nothing in an offhand way, in a mediocre manner.'

As the former Bishop of Oxford, Richard Harries, has said of Fr Alexander, 'He was nothing if not Christ-centred and Christ-committed.' He believed that the Incarnate Christ can and should transform the entirety of human life. 'There is no such thing as the secular,' he claimed; the aim of Christianity is 'the churching of the world'. His approach was essentially world-affirming. He did not construct barriers but built bridges. This is evident in the generous and positive attitude that he adopted towards non-Orthodox Christian communities and indeed towards non-Christian faiths (in contrast to the viewpoint of all too many Orthodox believers, especially in Russia). At the same time, he was firmly loyal to Orthodoxy, and he always insisted upon the uniqueness of Christ.

One of Fr Alexander's master-themes was the value of the human person and the crucial significance of personal freedom. As he put it, 'Someone asked the philosopher Nicolas Berdyaev the paradoxical question: "Can God create a stone that He Himself could not move?" And Berdyaev promptly answered: "Yes, that stone is man."' Fr Alexander noted, 'God does not present Himself to us in a compellingly obvious way.' An act of faith is required; and faith presupposes freedom.

Readers of the present work will appreciate why Fr Alexander is coming to be recognized, far beyond Russia, as one of the most remarkable Christians of the twentieth century. Many go further than this, and see in him *par excellence* the man of the twenty-first century.

Metropolitan Kallistos of Diokleia

PREFACE

T HE MAN WHOSE life and witness are presented in
these pages is 'a priest for our time'. What do
we mean by this statement? As a disciple of the
Master who died on the cross, Alexander Men carried
his apostolate right through to the end. Fully conscious
of the threats hanging over him he sacrificed his life in
advance, never ceasing to preach the Good News. His
youth coincided with the dark years of Stalinism and
the Second World War. Then, following an uncom-
pleted period of university study, he entered the
priesthood, under a regime which sought to suppress
every expression of religious faith.

But might one not be tempted here to draw a
parallel with ourselves? For life here in the West, both
in the political—or rather politically correct—and
economic spheres (the obsession with wealth), and in
the moral sphere (an unbridled laxity), has brought
about a situation in which God, however central to the
lives of a great many Christians, has been pushed to
the side-lines. This has come about, admittedly, not
through measures of violence: priests are not shot as

in the days of Stalin, and believers are not interned in psychiatric asylums as in the time of Brezhnev. It has happened in a covert, particularly insidious manner, which has sought to brand those who contemplate the beauty of the spiritual world as oddballs or fanatics, even mentally retarded. 'I never think about God', the well-known novelist Françoise Sagan once stated, indicating, even so, that God was still part of her mental framework. But when a youngster looking round a museum stops in front of a painting of the Virgin Mary and exclaims: 'Who's that lady with a baby on her knees?' one feels a terrible dislocation, a stunned bewilderment in the face of this ignorance about God. The void is growing, cutting young people off from their cultural roots.

During the decades when Russians were being brainwashed into believing that God does not exist, this was the void which Father Men was called on to fill, through the intelligence of his witness, through the warm welcome he offered to the crowds of people searching for God, and through his openness to every area of culture. He did not shut himself away in a cramped ecclesiastical environment but breathed the air of the open sea, even though he was forbidden to travel, and his reputation drew to his modest church Christians from far and wide, people like Cardinal Lustiger and Jean Vanier. Whilst in France today there is a natural respect for the Muslim or Jewish religions, the Christian religion seems open to every sort of mockery and distortion, and without any redress. Alexander Men's own words, which echo those of Pope John Paul II, may be quoted here: 'Do not be afraid'; they serve as a reminder to ourselves that it is the Christian's lot to be ridiculed, like Christ on the

Cross; yet the Christian is also capable of saying: 'Father, forgive them...'

Michel Evdokimov

1

At that time a great persecution arose against the Church (Ac 8:1)

F ATHER ALEXANDER MEN liked this thought of Master Eckart: 'God's word is spoken in silence.' There is God's silence, from which his Word issued, and there is the silence imposed by men in order to suppress the Word. Alexander Men came into the world in 1935 at the height of the Stalin persecutions aimed at suppressing every expression of religious feeling, one of those convulsive moments of history when man seeks to make himself god. Fifty-five years later, early one Sunday morning as the priest was making his way to church to celebrate the Liturgy, he was brutally assassinated by an axe which struck him down from behind. There were those who were determined to reduce his voice to silence. But his voice continues to be heard through his many writings, strengthening the waverers and reviving a flame of hope, not only amongst Russian readers but also amongst readers abroad, and forging bonds of communion with a philosophy or train of thought developed through long years of trial, and still astonishingly alive today.

Spare your people, O Lord! (Jl 2:17)

Ever since the country's baptism in 988 marking the birth of the Russian nation and State, the Church has been present at the different, often painful stages of Russia's history. During the two centuries following, the Church rapidly assimilated the liturgical traditions and literary texts of Byzantium. But in the thirteenth century, the splendid flowering of the civilization and spirituality of Kiev was trampled underfoot by the Mongol hordes who destroyed, burned and pillaged everything in their path. The Church, against all odds, held the country together and became the mouthpiece of the national consciousness so severely shaken by the ordeals. In the fourteenth century Moscow, which had now become the capital, was invested with the mission of uniting the Russian territories. During the course of a famous battle, Grand Prince Dmitri Donskoy succeeded in conquering the armies of the Mongol khan and so restored the morale of a severely weakened nation which, a century later, would free itself for all times from the Tartar yoke. Before pitting his strength against the Mongol armies, Dmitri Donskoy had gone to seek the blessing of Saint Sergius of Radonezh—as he was to be known—both for himself and the Russian troops. In this way an alliance was forged between Church and State to save the people from their intolerable suffering and to restore in them a sense of well-being. This was the landscape of desolation in which there emerged the luminous figure of Saint Sergius who built the famous Monastery of the Trinity, not far from Moscow, under the protective shadow of which Alexander Men was to spend several years of his life. During this same period numerous disciples of Sergius went out into vast areas of northern Russia, clearing forests, drawing peasants after them, and working as colonisers (with no political overtones).

The fall of Constantinople in 1453 was a great shock to people's minds. They felt themselves invested with a new messianic role, which a monk from Pskov, Philotheus, expressed in terms of 'the third Rome': the first had fallen into heresy, the second under the onslaughts of the Turks, and the third, Moscow, remained on its own to take up the challenge; there would not be a fourth. The religious philosopher Soloviev noted that Russia had kept her distance from the schism between the first and second Rome, and liked to think that because of this she would have a particular role to play when the moment for reconciliation came.

The relations between Church and State attempted to model themselves on the Byzantine 'symphony', in which the spiritual power of the patriarch and the temporal power of the emperor achieved harmony between them. In Russia, the alliance between throne and altar was brutally terminated in the sixteenth century by Ivan the Terrible, when he had the metropolitan Philip of Moscow murdered because he had dared to stand up to him and defend the people against the acts of violence and bloodshed perpetrated by his militias. Later, the split between Old Believers and those who were loyal to the official Church led Tsar Alexis to introduce measures to maintain the unity of the Church.

The most spectacular reform was instituted by Peter the Great. Anxious to open up his country to the nations of the West, he forced the Orthodox Church to model itself, administratively, on the Lutheran churches. The last patriarch, Adrian, died in 1700 without a successor. The Church was then governed by a synod with a collegial directorate of twelve members presided over by a high procurator from the laity.

This arbitrary step taken by the tsar raised the ecclesiological problem of the way in which the Church should be governed. The Roman Church had chosen the path of centralism and forged its unity around a head, the successor to Peter, who had executive authority over his Church worldwide. At the opposite extreme, the Churches which came out of the Reformation opted for an approach in which the sole authority resided in the Word of the Scriptures, attested to by the Holy Spirit working in the believer. The latter retained a wide freedom of interpretation, and this resulted in a proliferation of Churches of great diversity.

The operational principle of the Orthodox Church is collegiality, balanced by a hierarchical organisation which, in the final resort, assumes responsibility for decisions at every level, the patriarchate, the diocese and the parish. This operating principle derives from a theological interpretation of the Trinity, presented as the perfect model of government. The Holy Trinity is in fact both monarchical and collegial. It is monarchical in the sense that the Father is the source or fount of all divinity. From Him the Son was begotten, who obeyed Him until death on the Cross, to repeat the words of Saint Paul; from Him proceeded the Holy Spirit who taught all things to men (Jn 14:26). It is collegial in the sense that the Three Persons are united in one nature and conduct their actions in perfect harmony. This is what Andrei Rublev represented in the icon of the Holy Trinity. The three angels of the Grand Council are deliberating about whom they will send to fulfil the work of the Incarnation. Christ becomes man in conformity with the will of the Father, and in accordance with the Holy Spirit which descends on him at his baptism in the Jordan and never leaves him for the rest of his mission on earth. Saint Irenaeus said that the Son and the Spirit were 'the two hands of the Father' in the action of the divinity turned towards the world.

The icon of the Trinity is thus the guiding image of the way in which the Church's governance should operate and decisions be taken. This is attested to by an ancient canon according to which the bishop is conceived first as an absolute Monarch, then, subsequently, is beholden never to take a decision without referring to the collegial assembly around him so that, in the final resort, the Holy Trinity may be glorified. We have here an ideal image to which ecclesiastical institutions are invited to conform, these however, like all human institutions, subject to their own weaknesses and contradictions. The ideal remains under tension in a realization which is never final.

What, then, was the sign of unity in a universal Church deprived of a sovereign pontiff to whom the bishops owed allegiance? It was embodied in the Liturgy as celebrated throughout the world, in the person of Christ manifested in his broken body and spilled blood, the sole head of the Church which he accompanies on its journey towards the Kingdom.

The council of 1917–1918 involved the Russian Orthodox Church in a series of reforms akin to those of Vatican II. © D.R.

Even though Peter the Great's abolition of the patriarchate was an anti-canonical act, it did not destroy the core truth, the symbolic unity affirmed through the Eucharist between the Russian Church and all other Orthodox patriarchates.

As a result of the Emperor's despotic policy, the Church was thus transformed into an organ of State of which the tsar was now the head, and the predominance of the temporal power over the spiritual was legitimised. The reform resulted in the bureaucratisation of ecclesiastical life. Then it was the turn of Catherine II, an admirer of the philosophers of the Enlightenment, to display her power by abolishing more than half of the monasteries and confiscating their lands to the benefit of the State. In this way she deprived the monastic communities of the role they had always played in the fields of hospitality and charity.

Despite the increased bureaucracy in the official Church, the current of sainthood and prophecy flowed on undiminished. Saint Tikhon of Zadonsk, whom Dostoevsky used as the model of a bishop open to modernity; Saint Païssi, the translator of the Philokalia, who contributed to a renewal of religious faith through prayer and asceticism; Saint Seraphim of Sarov, an apostle of inner peace in a life illuminated by the flame of the Holy Spirit; the *Startsi* of the monastery of Optino frequented by politicians and peasants, rich merchants and famous writers in search of the living word: all of these testify to the fact that the aspiration towards saintliness was as strong as ever.[2] To this list should be added a remarkable

---

[2]   In the Russian Orthodox church, *Startsi* (plural) are elders or spiritual teachers from whom younger monks take advice and orders. St Seraphim of Sarov was the original and most famous *Starets*.

missionary venture to Siberia (a continent in itself!), and to Alaska and Japan. And finally, there was Father John of Kronstadt, a priest in a working-class parish, who was well-known as a miracle worker. Alexander Men's great-grandmother, a widow with seven children to look after, was suffering from a serious illness and was advised by friends to go and see the priest when he was passing through the town. She followed their advice. After staring at her for a moment, Father John said: 'I know you are a Jew, but I see in you a profound faith in God. Let us pray to the Lord, and He will heal you.' A month later she was in good health again. Only saintliness as illustrated by these examples — and many more could be cited — could have kept alive the free flow of the spiritual forces from which the future Father Alexander was to benefit; it alone could have fostered the discipline of mind essential to the creative life, and the opening to grace which allows God to 'make all things new' (Rev 21:5).

The fall of the monarchy in 1917 made possible the convocation of the Council of Moscow, which was to break up a year later. It brought home to the Russian Church a new reality: the sudden disappearance of the Christian Empire, one of whose missions had been to 'protect' the Church. It was a question now of learning to live without this 'protection', of learning to develop relations — sometimes paid for with one's blood - with the Bolshevik rule, which had written into its programme, defined along Leninist lines, the destruction of all expressions of religious sentiment. The first State founded upon atheism came into being amidst the most terrible suffering: waves of persecution, arbitrary trials, deportations to the camps, the pitiless destruction of churches and monasteries or their conversion into garages, dance halls or prisons, like the famous monastery on the Solovki Islands in the Far North. The separation between Church and State, written into the Constitution, was never observed by the State which permanently subjected the Church to close police surveillance, of which Father Alexander Men was many times a victim. The hierarchy was partly recruited to defend the political interests of the Soviet power on the international scene. The voices of those who dared to protest, whether priests or lay people, were systematically repressed.

Then came the year 1988, which marked the millennium of Russia's baptism. The spiritual patrimony accumulated over the centuries, which the Soviet authorities had tried to cover up for seventy-five years, was able to manifest itself anew, and there were fresh glimmers of hope. During the period of *glasnost*, minds were opened to the real world, and in the face of the decadence of the totalitarian State, the Church began to come into its own again and catechesis was allowed. Father Alexander was the first to perform this openly. With the fall of the totalitarian system, tens of thousands of people asked to be baptised. Charitable activity, banned during the period when the communist party was supposed to provide for all of people's needs, was able to resume, albeit in conditions of material and financial hardship, yet with immense commitment and dedication; for poverty, the abandonment of children by broken families, alcoholism and prostitution were spreading at an alarming rate.

Patriarch Alexis articulated the Church's repentance for the faults it had committed, notably Metropolitan Sergius's declaration of allegiance in 1927 to the Soviet Union and its leaders. This declaration was an offence to the martyrs to the faith, even if it had been an attempt to safeguard what could be safeguarded of the visibility of the Church and so prevent it from being driven underground.

At the present time, however, Russia's adaptation to a new stage in its history is not running particularly smoothly. There are various forces to contend with: ingrained reactions from the Soviet period with its totalitarian utopia promising to forge a 'new man', yet which has left people in a state of total disarray; an instinctive rejection of capitalist society, yet without there being any clear conception, after the fall of collectivism, of what can take its place; an attitude of irrational opposition to the West which, it is true, has spread the corrosive influence of money, drugs, pornography, and moral laxity, yet has demonstrated too the values of democracy and tolerance; reactions of misunderstanding and mistrust with regard to Western forms of Christianity, with which, however, the Orthodox Church has such treasures of spirituality to share, this in a Europe which is turning away from its Judaeo-Christian roots and is succumbing to an attitude of general indifference. It has to be admitted that the mass incursion of American 'missionaries' laden with cases full of dollars, and the blunders of the Vatican, not to mention Catholic fundamentalists who come and plant themselves in the country as though it were a heathen land waiting for conversion, then the regrettable quarrels about Uniatism, have all had a deeply disturbing effect on people's minds.[3] This is why Pope John Paul II was unable to realize the

---

[3] Uniatism is the union of an Eastern Rite Church with the See of Rome in which the authority of the Papacy is accepted without loss of separate liturgies or government by local patriarchs.

project, so close to his heart, of visiting Russia and renewing dialogue with representatives of its Church. Even so, there is a great tribute to be paid to all those Christians from the West who go to Russia to help their fellow humans with the reconstruction of their country and to organize exchanges in a spirit of comradeship and generosity. And there is the reverse movement, when groups of young Russians are welcomed into Western communities, like the one at Taizé, which was especially close to Father Alexander's heart.

All in all, Russia is to be seen as a country in which the feeling for religion is fairly widespread but lacks a solid structural foundation, and in which religious observance remains weak. Whilst attitudes persist from the period of the concordat with the tsar—to which a minority would like to return—and from the uncertain period when totalitarianism exercised its intolerable power, the Church today has to go through a difficult apprenticeship of separation from the State. It has to find its way independently, illuminated by the saints who have shed their light over the Russian soil and kept alive the flame of faith, in communion with the people and their leaders, but also in the total freedom of children of God, free from subjection to the powers of this world.

See how my enemies have humiliated me (Ps 9:13)

Already at the end of the nineteenth century a number of enlightened minds had realized the need for the Russian Church to carry out its *aggiornamento*. This was before the Catholic Church had Vatican II. However, it was not until 1917 that a council assembled in Moscow. It managed to come up with a series of important measures, but under the pressure of new political forces it was forced to break up in 1918, before completing its work. Right up until the present day these measures have remained a dead letter. The Church entered a period of darkness whose shadows even today have barely lifted. The saints, however, those from the past as well as those in our own time—and there are already voices demanding the canonization of Father Alexander Men—are always there, and their light will shine till the end of time, for against the Church the gates of hell can not prevail.

The Bolshevik regime lost no time in entering into open conflict with the Church. The era of persecutions started. A large number of churches were converted into warehouses or dance halls or were razed to the ground, and today they are being rebuilt, sometimes identical to the original, like the Cathedral of Christ the Saviour in Moscow. However, it is an infinitely more delicate task to rebuild, not churches in stone, but churches in the flesh, those 'temples of the Holy Spirit' that are human beings. Under Stalin, tens of thousands of bishops, priests and believers were imprisoned in concentration camps or shot. During the period from the Revolution to the War, the number of martyrs to the faith far exceeded those who died during the first three centuries of Christianity. In 1925, the patriarch Tikhon, later to be canonized, died in strange circumstances. In 1927, his successor made a declaration of loyalty to the Soviet power. Some looked upon this as a betrayal, as compromise with the power of 'the prince of this world'; others saw in his act a concern to preserve what could be preserved of the Church's visibility, and so prevent its disappearance from the face of men. Some priests refused to conform and abandoned their parishes or went into hiding, taking refuge in houses well away from prying eyes. If denounced, they were eliminated on the spot. They belonged to the underground Church, the Church of the catacombs.

This was the Church, with its turbulent historical backcloth, into which Alik (an affectionate diminutive for Alexander) was born and grew into the faith.

2

The child grew and the Lord blessed him (Jg 13:24)

Many shall rejoice at his birth (Lk 1:14)

TWO FAIRY GODMOTHERS presided over Alik's birth, his mother, Elena Semionovna, and Elena's sister, Vera Iakovlevna, who was part of the family and shared fully in its life. The two sisters enjoyed a close, affectionate relationship, and the aunt was entrusted in particular with the education of Alik and of his brother Paul. A few years previously, the two women had made the acquaintance of a priest remarkable for his courage and his unshakeable faith. This was Father Seraphim (Batioukov). He had already been arrested on a false denunciation then released. He had received the tonsure in the twenties, the period when Christians were the object of systematic persecution by the authorities. To safeguard his personal freedom and escape the brutalities of the Soviet police, he had become a dissident and exercised his ministry clandestinely, in 'the Church of the catacombs'. To this end he had taken up residence in a small house not far from the Monastery of the Trinity. It was here, in 1935, that he baptised Elena and her son who was then seven months old. The latter was given the name Alexander, in honour of Grand Prince Alexander Nevsky, who in the eleventh century had defended the integrity of the Russian territory and the Orthodox faith against the plots of the Swedes and Teutonic knights. His aunt Vera, a more tormented soul, was not baptised until two years later. His father remained a non-believer but, in the words of Saint Paul, in a couple like this 'the non-believing husband is sanctified by the wife' (1 Co 7:14). The latter did not worry on her husband's account because, she said, 'the Lord saves the humble' (Ps 34:18).

When he was almost four, Alik was taken to a celebration of the Liturgy conducted in a remote forest clearing by another priest of the catacombs, Father Ieraks. This is how Vera Iakovlevna described the occasion: 'The forest had become a church. All the hosts of the woods seemed to raise a song of praise to the Mother of God. A squirrel came down from a tree and kept us company, remaining all the while perfectly still.' The small boy said to his uncle some time later, still stirred by the event: 'What a pity you weren't with us. It was so marvellous!'

His love of the forest and animals and of the whole of nature may have dated from this time. He would say later that when he entered a forest, it was with the same feeling of awe as when he entered a church. Through the windows of the sanctuary where he celebrated the Liturgy, he was moved by the sense of God's presence in the spectacle of the fields turning green in spring, or white under the winter snow. The remark of Sherpa Tensing on his ascent of Everest with

Hillary, 'mountains are to be approached with veneration', made a deep impression on him.

His mother instilled in him the notion of God the Creator of the universe, whose love was outpoured on all. One day, hearing someone speak of the fear of God, he asked: 'We love God, so how can we fear him?' His mother answered: 'We must be afraid of offending him by a bad action.' This idea pacified him.

Instruct the child in the way he should go (Pr 22:6)

Vera, the aunt, spent her free time taking the child for walks, and whilst he was quietly playing she would devote herself to prayer. When Alik was in his fifth year, Father Seraphim recommended that he be introduced to the Scriptures. Neither the mother nor aunt, despite their deep faith, felt equal to the task. So they turned to a friend who was more experienced in the field of religious instruction, Maria Vitalievna, who was herself a spiritual daughter of Father Seraphim. Later, the roles would be reversed and the catechist, now a member of Father Alexander's parish, would be indebted to him for his spiritual teaching. The first words the boy wrote in his exercise book, probably under her dictation, were: 'Overcome evil with good' (Rm 12:21). On Father Seraphim's advice, the child was taken to neither the cinema nor the theatre, for they were places of falsehood and of atheist ideology. 'You'd be better buying him a toy', the priest suggested.

On the outbreak of war, Vera organised the family's move to Serguiev Possad (called at the time Zagorsk). Father Seraphim had stated that in Moscow 'children could perish, whereas here Saint Sergius would protect them'. He had a particular liking for Alik, and with his keen sense of discernment said to Vera one day: 'Thanks to your efforts and all you have put into his education, Alik is destined for a great future.' When the war was over, Vera took her adolescent nephew to visit a number of monasteries. Almost everywhere he went he attracted the attention of some perceptive monk who intuitively sensed the great future awaiting him, both as a man and a priest.

Alik's mother was struck down by galloping consumption, and doctors predicted she had only a few months to live. She survived for several more years, however, and did not die until 1979. Those who knew her believed it was God's will that her life should be sustained, she was so full of vitality, joy and peace. Her heart overflowed with love, which she communicated to all she met. Even when she was ill she radiated a *joie de vivre* and would express gratitude for the smallest acts of kindness shown to her, and she was always ready to sit down and talk with those who needed her. Despite the food shortages, she always managed to conjure up a meal for their many visitors. Everyone was overwhelmed by the atmosphere of love she radiated. It was thanks to her and her sister that Alik caught the flame of faith.

Feeling his end approaching, Father Seraphim did not wait for Alik to attain the statutory age of seven to hear his first confession. After the event, premature as it was, the boy said to his mother and aunt: 'With grandfather I felt as though I was in heaven with God.' On the eve of his death, in 1942, Father Seraphim blessed the boy with an icon of the Mother of God called 'Joy of all the afflicted'.

Another character from the catacombs who crossed Alik's destiny was Mother Mary. She was a sister of the great vesture—the highest monastic rank for men as well as for women—with the title of *higoumenia*, indicating she was qualified to run a monastery, as abbess. She too lived in hiding, and was very perceptive. One day, catching sight of Alik through her cell window as he was opening the garden gate, she exclaimed, half serious, half joking: 'Ah, here comes the father archimandrite!' She had the premonition that he would one day take holy orders. The young man did not become a monk, however, (the archimandrite is the superior of a monastery) for he married before being ordained. During the fifties and sixties a large number of priests turned to Mother Mary for help, seeking her advice on how to carry out their duties and asking her to help them through her prayers. The future Father Alexander retained grateful memories of her radiating personality, which had brought such succour to him whilst she was alive. He made a point of visiting her house each year on the anniversary of her death. She died in 1961, in her eighty-first year.

One of the many talents Alik was gifted with was painting. At the age of sixteen he did a composition in oils of the prophet Ezekiel, which was almost prophetic in tone. The huge figure of God's herald, his beard and hair caught by the wind, is silhouetted against a stormy sky across which scud threatening clouds, with black crows hovering. Human bones are scattered over the ground, and one can almost hear the roar of God's voice: 'Prophesy, son of man, and say to the Spirit: come, breathe upon the slain, that they may live' (Ez 37:9). A few years later, the young man entered the priesthood. To how many 'dried bones' did he not himself restore a taste for life through his inspiring words, the warmth of his love, the breadth of his compassion? The bones took on new flesh, their hearts beat faster and were resonant with hope; they could start on a new path in life, in the service of God and their fellow men.

The prophet Ezekiel.
Painting by Alexander Men (1950). © D. R.

When he was still a schoolboy, Alik showed a particular predilection for the offices of the Liturgy. One New Year's Eve after the Vigil Service, when everyone else was already outside preparing to welcome the New Year in, he had remained behind in the church. Suddenly he felt the priest's hand on him, and the priest said: 'It's good that you love God, the Church and the celebration of the Liturgy. But you will never become a true pastor if you remain detached from the joys and afflictions of those in the world...' These words opened up entirely new horizons for him. He continued to pursue his own thoughts for a while, then he walked out of the church filled with an inexpressible joy and the feeling that Someone was calling him. He was a new man. He could feel the vocation taking shape in him to be with those who suffer and mourn, with those who are on the threshold of death or are without faith, hope and love, as too to be with those who rejoice.

Ezra had prepared his heart to seek the law of the Lord (Ezr 7:10)

Alik was a precocious boy and he began to write articles when he was barely twelve. He subjected himself to a harsh discipline, going to bed early and getting up at dawn to study, when all was quiet and everyone else in the house was still asleep. Time was precious and had to be turned to good account. He struggled against intellectual as well as spiritual laziness. 'The person who frees himself frees the world', he was in the habit of saying. This freedom from the burden of selfhood, which remains the overriding preoccupation of so many, enabled him to devote himself to his neighbour and bring him comfort and help, always with the utmost patience, tolerance and capacity for love.

In 1953 he enrolled at a university institute in Moscow specializing in biology, which shortly afterwards moved to Irkutsk. He was thus free to devote himself to his favourite subject, biology, and to study the life and habits of animals for which he had a real passion. His library was full of books on the subject. Even dinosaurs—whose direct descendants he claimed were hens, following the lead of other scientists—occupy an important place in his animal drawings. Sometimes children would come rushing into his room and bombard him with questions on the ways and habits of the animal world.

Gifted with a musical ear and a rich, vibrant voice, he started very early on singing in the choir and assumed the duties of reader. He liked the beauty of ceremonial, but never allowed himself to be caught up in aestheticism. Singing, architecture, the books of the liturgy and the maintenance of tradition occupied, it is true, an important place in his heart, but he acknowledged at the same time that all of these things were ephemeral and of hardly more importance than the traditions of the ancient Egyptians or Hindus, if one did not feel the presence of Christ and hear his voice more clearly than all the rest.

The extent of his reading and the number of authors he was able to quote were strikingly rich and diverse. It remains a mystery how he managed to obtain such a large number of books, published in Russia as well as in the West, many of which were unobtainable or banned under the Soviet regime. One can only assume that a network of friends travelling between Paris and Moscow devised all the means they could of satisfying his hunger for books. The Russian Revolution had put a stop to every expression of free creative thinking, also within the theological sphere. Only the well-known Russian theologians of the emigration, in particular at the Saint-Serge Institute in Paris, were able with the limited means at their disposal to compensate for this vacuum of religious thought in their native country. Father Alexander was one of the very few theologians of the Soviet period who managed one way or another to keep up with what was being published in the West.

Amongst the great religious thinkers who exercised a profound influence over him during the years of his intellectual and spiritual formation was Nicolas Berdyaev, for whom Christianity was the revelation of the person in the mystery of its inalienable liberty. Meditating on the meaning of history, the philosopher maintained that the tragic in life can only be resolved on the plane of the Spirit. Alexander Men understood full well that communism could not be combated with violence, but only by spiritual means, through the transformation of people's hearts. Vladimir Soloviev, for his part, opened his mind to the idea of a closer relationship between Churches, and to Christian unity. Father Alexander did not share the pessimism the philosopher felt at the end of his life, discouraged as he was by the negligible results of his efforts, in a nineteenth century characterized, it is true, by the jealously self-protectionist and inward-looking attitude of its Churches. Soloviev was at this time a prey to dark eschatological visions in which he saw the unity of the Churches being realized only at the ultimate moment of the *Parousia*—Christ's second coming at the end of the world. Alexander Men, on the other hand, felt that Christianity was only at its beginning and he had an optimistic vision of historical evolution, reminiscent in certain respects of Teilhard de Chardin. Father Serge Bulgakov, who was the first dean of the Saint-Serge Institute in Paris, provided him with the framework of dogma he needed in order to establish his theological vision on solid foundations.

A promising theologian had during these years little possibility of exercising creativity in his studies, or of publishing works in his discipline. Seminaries were poorly equipped, and teaching was dispensed mechanically from nineteenth century textbooks which ignored the questions preoccupying a contemporary mind. As was always the case in periods of trouble and persecution, only the Liturgical Offices, with their inexhaustible riches, could preserve the elevation of mind and spiritual nourishment of those who participated in them. Men had to create his own language, through his writings and lectures, in order to convey a living representation of the Christian faith. He wrote his *Jesus, the Master of Nazareth*, for example, in such a way as to make its message accessible to readers from a non-Christian background, but without making any compromises in the presentation of the truth.

Whilst at university, the young man continued as before his services to the Church as a cantor and reader. He was playing with fire, for the educational system was under close surveillance to avoid any infiltration of religious influences. A student found participating in the life of the Church was liable to the most severe punishments. It was right at the end of his course, the day before he sat his final examination, that this brilliant student was expelled from the University by order of the supervising authorities. Thus he never received his degree from the Institute of Biology. From now on, his life was to take a totally different course.

Alexander Men and his mother. © D. R.

3

The law shall not perish for want of priests (Jr 18:18)

D URING THE WAR, in order to resist the German invader, Stalin had no option but to mobilize all the energies of the nation, in particular the sense of patriotism of the Russian people. He relaxed his repressive hold on the Church, and it was allowed to reopen some of the parishes which had been closed after the Revolution. In 1953 Lenin's successor died, and it was the start of an era characterized by a new air of freedom: the thaw. But soon, under Khrushchev, the anti-religious campaign flared up again worse than ever and parishes, one after the other, were ordered to cease their activities. An icy chill blew over the land. Then, dissident circles began to spring up and, through their questioning of the nature of the society being formed under a totalitarian regime, began to shape public opinion. Amongst these 'people who [thought] differently'—that is how they were designated—was Solzhenitsyn, whose short novel *A Day in the Life of Ivan Denisovich*, appearing in 1962, created a sensation.

He restored an image of the grandeur and nobility of man (even if, like the hero, he was from the peasant class), of man endowed with consciousness and capable, paradoxically, of retaining his inner freedom in the inhuman conditions of incarceration in a concentration camp. He revealed to the whole country the reality of life in the Gulags, the most glaring crime of the regime. Later, the famous scientist Sakharov stood up as the defender of freedom of conscience and human rights.

Alexander Men belonged to the generation of young people who grew up during the war and experienced the Stalinist period when it was in decline; they were not taken in by the political rhetoric of the ideology in power. Many of them went into higher education and questioned the meaning of life and of God; some of them started attending church again and were even baptised. Certain priests such as Dmitri Dudko, known in the West for his spiritual dialogues with members of his Church, baptised people in their hundreds if not thousands. Even Stalin's daughter, Svetlana Alliluieva, plunged into the lustral waters! Contrary to what was happening in the West, where members of the intellectual classes were often devotees of secularism and anticlericalism, in Russia it was amongst the intelligentsia that were to be found young people who agonized over what Dostoevsky called the 'accursed questions': what is the meaning of life, death, suffering and love, and where does God fit into it all? Sensitive to this changed outlook and new search for truth and meaning, Alexander Men realized how ill-equipped the Church was to deal with the situation and how urgent it was to find the means of adapting to it.

He was called to enter the temple of the Lord (Lk 1:9)

Following his expulsion from the Institute of Biology, Alexander Men started studying theology. He enrolled on correspondence courses with the seminary at Leningrad, and subsequently completed the advanced course of study at the Academy of Theology in Moscow. In 1958 he was ordained a deacon, then two years later, a priest. He wrote articles which were published in the *Journal of the Patriarchate of Moscow*, the only periodical of the Russian church in existence, numerous issues of which, even so, were unobtainable in Russia and were sent to the West.

The first parish where he was appointed rector was at Alabino, a small town not far from the capital. He established good relations with both the local authorities and the parishioners. He got on well with his auxiliary, Father Sergius Khoklov. 'We enjoyed celebrating the Liturgy together,' he stated retrospectively of this period of his life. He was overflowing with energy, and devoted himself untiringly to the church's restoration as well as to his many activities as a priest: preaching, confessions, and spiritual guidance to his parishioners. Appalled by the state of neglect and tawdriness of so many religious buildings, he kept a close eye on the style of icons and on questions of interior decoration. Right up to the end of his life he would attach great importance to the appearance of God's house.

Sadly, the novice priest was to experience one misfortune after another. His parishioners, mostly local people and intellectuals who made the journey from the capital, were inspired by the depth of his preaching. But a minority turned against him, stirred up by the civil authorities who had control over the parish and were as suspicious as ever, and also by the religious authorities, jealous of the success of their younger colleague. A cabal organized against him on trumped-up evidence resulted in a police raid on the small house which served as presbytery. Orders were given to scrutinize all the books, manuscripts and other papers, to ensure they did not contain any 'anti-Soviet material'. Whilst the search was going on, the young priest—now twenty-six—anxious not to fritter away any of his time, completed the final pages of his *Magic and Monotheism*, the second volume of a work which was to run to six volumes, entitled *In Search of the Way, the Truth, and the Life*.

Throughout his life, this exceptional man was subjected to one false accusation after another, and had to submit to searches of his premises or appear before judicial interrogators who sometimes detained him for hours on end. A friend once asked him: 'Was it hard?' and he replied: 'Well, I'm a priest, you know, and it's my job to speak to anyone. It's never hard for me.'

The denunciations eventually served their purpose. Father Alexander was transferred, with the status of third priest, to the church of Tarassovka. This small town, situated on the line from Moscow to Serguiev Possad, also served Semkhoz, and it was there that he lived with his wife and their two children. The move seemed propitious, for it was not far from the spot where some six hundred years earlier, in what was then a dark forest infested with wolves, Saint Sergius of Radonezh had shone forth in all his saintly splendour.

In the courtyard of Alabino Abbey, 1964. Photo © Victor Andreev.

But this new appointment turned out to be as disastrous as the previous one. He had to endure continual humiliations from the rector of the parish as well as face up to endless false accusations. Yet he was impervious to all the slander and malice, consumed by an inner joy as he saw his flock growing, mostly made up of young people and intellectuals. The situation became untenable, however, and the patriarch, Pimen, decided to transfer him once again, this time — and it was to be the last — to the Church of the Holy Meeting at Novaya Derevnia. This village was close to the town of Pouchkino, and was on the same railway line as his previous parish. Years later, he would look back upon the patriarch's decision to move him with the utmost gratitude.

In the true tradition of the Church, a priest is 'married' to his parish and he must not show infidelity by moving elsewhere, unless for reasons beyond his control. Father Alexander made these moves against his will. Everywhere he went, however, he radiated the intelligence and beauty of the Christian faith. At that time a good priest was the worst enemy of an aggressively atheistic regime, for he made religion attractive, whilst the aim was to destroy it by every means possible. Like a flock of crows, dark forces were closing in on a pastor with a pure heart, dedicated to his flock.

The number of those who believed in the Lord increased (Ac 5:14)

On the feast day of the three doctor saints — Saint Basil, Saint Gregory the Theologian, and Saint John Chrysostom — 2 February 1970, Men assumed his duties at

the Church of the Holy Meeting. The church, sur-
mounted by a blue cupola, was modest in size and
constructed of wood, with a flight of steps leading up
to it. In the courtyard was a small wooden house used
by the priest, where he could receive a few visitors,
and there was a cemetery. Men carried out his ministry
there for twenty years, in a spirit of total dedication,
until that famous Sunday of 9 September 1990 when
he made the supreme sacrifice of his life.

The close members of his family, his mother, aunt,
wife and children, played an active part in the life of
the parish. But the 'family' given to him by God was
enlarged by his numerous spiritual progeny. He was
always a devoted father who took an active interest in
each member of his family, yet at the same time his
whole being was dedicated to Christ, who always took
first place. A married priest with a family has to find
a balance between the time devoted to his family and
the time devoted to the 'children' he has to bring up
spiritually. His wife, who was affectionately known as
'Matushka' (the priest himself was called 'Baty-
oushka') worked for a living.[4] Her husband helped her
with the housework, prepared meals on occasions, and
took the washing to the laundry.

He was naturally drawn to children, perhaps
because in spirit he had never ceased to be a child
himself. One day he would be with a group of adoles-
cents, projecting slides on the life of Christ; he would
comment on the slides and enjoy observing their
reactions. Another time he would be showing a set of
slides on the life of Jesus to a six-year-old all on its own,
and he would explain in detail to the child their

---

[4]   These are affectionate terms for mother and father, used of the
      priest and his wife.

meaning. On one occasion, after he had been author-
ized to visit hospitals, he spent the whole afternoon at
the bedside of a little girl suffering from an incurable
form of leukaemia.

However, false denunciations, slanderous letters
and crass accusations continued to rain down on this
luminous figure. They were the product of ignorance
and jealousy. He continued on his course, exercising
his ministry and closing his eyes to the torrents of mud
slung in his path. He was always on the alert, avoiding
confrontation with the authorities. His writings were
published under a pseudonym by the Foyer Oriental,
a Catholic organisation in Brussels. One day his friend,
Yves Hamant, the author of the first biography on
Men—still a key work—turned up at Novaya Derevnia
with one of his books which had been published in
Russian in Brussels; his laughter and joy were inde-
scribable when he saw where certain of the illustra-
tions had come from ... they were borrowings from
publications by militant atheists!

Right until 1988 persons looking for advice or comfort
would steal into Novaya Derevnia like conspirators,
unseen by the authorities. Their number increased from
year to year, so great was the priest's reputation. He had
the knack of putting himself on the same wavelength as
whoever he was speaking to, intuitively grasping from
the first moment of contact their state of mind, comfort-
ing them if they were distressed, bringing light to them
if they were struggling in the darkness. His reputation
spread throughout the Moscow region and even further
afield. Sometimes, a mere laying-on of hands alleviated
the suffering and symptoms of fear and anguish. When
he pronounced that 'the situation [was] difficult', it was
necessary to summon up patience, but there would

always be a solution in sight. In the most complicated cases, the words 'all is well' were like balm applied to wounds which were already beginning to heal.

The priest's personality itself, moreover, radiated joy; joy was a natural expression with him, entirely lacking in artifice. He said one should give oneself totally to the matter in hand, whether in the sphere of work, prayer, human relationships, or pleasure. He knew how to enjoy himself, whether recounting anecdotes, singing to his own accompaniment on the guitar, or joking with a group of 'babushki'[5] over a cup of tea. But above all he had the special gift of communicating to those who came to see him, perhaps in need of comfort, a feeling of deep, authentic joy which seemed to come from beyond himself. It was doubtless the same joy as bursts through so often in the gospels, especially following the Resurrection, and which inspired the disciples when Christianity was spreading throughout the world.

Two main tendencies can be discerned in Christianity. One is characterized by austerity, sadness, an inner torment in the face of all the evil there is in the world. The other reacts to life's contingencies with a radiant smile, and is always ready to bring comfort to the suffering and to spread joy. These two tendencies are represented symbolically by two characters in *The Brothers Karamazov* by Dostoevsky: the terrible monk Therapon, who sees devils everywhere and condemns humanity charged with the burden of sin, and the starets[6] Zossima who proclaims that love transforms the world into paradise and practises a ministry of compassion amidst those weighed down by suffering.

---

[5] A familiar, affectionate term for old ladies.

[6] A monk and spiritual adviser to lay people in a Russian monastery.

To help his parishioners, and especially the lonely, to grow in faith, Father Men created small groups of a dozen or so persons, called 'spiritual families'. At the head of each one he would place a person of experience, whom he also knew to be capable of finding a way round the obstacles created by an inquisitorial political system. These spiritual charges had to be on their guard, for they too were kept under close scrutiny by the police authorities. Father Men followed the groups' activities from a distance, and provided their leaders with books and advice on running the groups. He explained that just as a table rests on four legs, so the group rests on four principles: group prayer, group reading and commentary of the scriptures, frequent communion, and participation in charity and welfare work. In this way the Church's fabric was strengthened. One day Father Men had a vision: he saw before him the whole of his parish in prayer.

On each Sabbath all flesh shall come to worship before me (Is 66:23)

The church congregation at Novaya Derevnia was socially mixed. There were people from the country, ordinary peasants, side by side with young people, mostly intellectuals, from Moscow. Some people had no conception of what constituted correct behaviour in an Orthodox church and roused the indignation of the 'babushki', the old women or grandmothers who watched over the church with a severe eye. Father Alexander had the knack of putting these ordinary people at their ease and creating an atmosphere of tolerance and good humour. No-one was made to feel unwelcome.

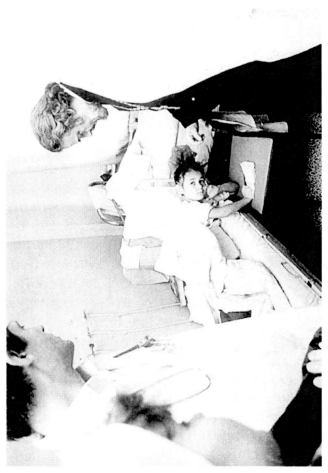

Visit to children stricken with leukaemia, January 1990.
Photo © Sergueï Bessmertmy.

He was well aware the authorities were watching him, also that members of the police came to listen to his sermons, but he would spot them immediately, for they had no idea how to conduct themselves in a church! The ecclesiastical authorities gave him a hard time too, for a successful priest arouses jealousies. The atmosphere of fear in which people had been living for decades—even members of the party were not immune—brought out the worst instincts in people, even amongst members of the parish council who had no qualms about sending letters of denunciation. But he remained impervious to it all and cleverly avoided the traps they laid for him.

On Sunday mornings throngs of worshippers would hasten to the church whilst others would be leaving; it was the usual hubbub prior to a service. In a side-section of the church, the priest would be explaining to a group of penitents the meaning of the sacrament of penitence and the need to confess to God all that burdens the soul and poisons relationships with one's fellows: anger, hostility, selfishness, everything, in short, which alienates one from the God of love. Everyone would kneel, the priest would put his stole on his head and pronounce the words of absolution in the name of the Lord who alone can confer pardon. Some would rise to their feet, their eyes lit up with joy. Many would come to ask for absolution; the dialogue would be only brief, but something powerful had been felt and they would return home, their faith strengthened and with a new feeling of hope. Sometimes the priest put his hand on a person's shoulder as a special sign of support and encouragement. His face would light up when a child came along.

Father Men had an exceptional memory for every detail of his penitents' lives. He gave everyone the impression they had a special place in his heart. One day someone spoke to him about how easily distracted he was during prayer; he replied that when praying, you have to force your way through. Another time, someone asked him how he could recognize what God's will for him was. Father Men advised him to examine his conscience and situation in life; the man did this, and found the answer he had been unable to find on his own. Finding salvation was not an egoistic act, but signified becoming one with God so as to make God known in the world. This was the meaning of the creative spirit Soloviev and Berdyaev spoke about.

Living in the permanent aura of God's presence, Father Alexander found in the Liturgy a natural extension of his life and activities, and an inexhaustible source from which to draw his energy. He had a gift for turning people's hearts towards Christ so they would go out personally to meet Him. The divine office was an act which laity and priest celebrated together. Whilst still part of this world, the worshippers' inner eye was turned towards the Kingdom to come, where they could 'lay aside all the cares of the world'. The communicants pressed in great numbers around the Eucharist, for Father Men insisted on the importance of frequent communion, at least once a month, as too on the importance of preparing for it properly, so there was no risk of trivialization. The sermon, which he prepared with great care, would be a commentary on the Gospel, or explain the significance of the liturgical event being celebrated that day. The priest had a gift for explaining things clearly, in words which were easy to understand yet were rich with meaning and which found a way into the hearts of uneducated and educated people alike; for everyone sought nourishment from the beauty of the divinity. By the end of the Liturgy his eyes would be as though illuminated by the mysteries he had just celebrated.

On certain Sundays, one or more coffins, still open as is the Russian custom, would be brought into the church and censed by the priest. Members of the family, including children, would stand round them in an attitude of great simplicity; it was an occasion to participate in the Liturgy and take communion one last time in the presence of those who had died. Standing in front of the bereaved, the priest would speak of death as the passage to a new life and anticipation of the Last Judgment; he would point out the importance of preparing oneself for it in one's everyday life. One witness recounts that on one occasion he had to conduct the funeral of a six month old child, called Alexander like himself. What could one say, what words of consolation could one offer at such a moment? Without disguising the profound grief he felt with the parents, Father Men stated that 'the life of the child, so prematurely ended here on earth, had not ceased but continued beyond in heaven ... under the loving, solicitous gaze of the Lord of life...' It was as though he already saw the child in the bosom of the One who had taken his soul into his keeping.

After the coffins had been carried out, there would be a group of adults and children waiting to be baptised. The priest would appear once more and explain in simple, straightforward language the meaning of baptism and the ritual of purification by water, which was a passing of the 'old man'; then the meaning of anointing with holy oils, a gift of the infinite diversity of the charisms of the Holy Spirit; then the meaning of the cross which the newly baptised wore round the neck as the sign of self-renunciation and discipleship to the Lord of life. Every conversion to Christ involved repentance: how light the soul now felt!

Once the baptism was over, there would still be people standing around waiting. The priest would go off to his little house to receive visitors, and spend some time with each one of them. Everybody was welcome, Orthodox, Christians from other confessions, or people who were still searching. They would all squeeze into his tiny room. He would always find the right word, and everyone would fall under his spell. That is what he was there for: to transmit the rudiments of faith to these people who were so full of good will; but what a huge void had been left in traditional religious culture by decades of anti-religious persecution!

Then, suddenly, there were new arrivals: young couples asking to be married. He would take the first two by the hand and lead them off, laughing, to the church, explaining to them on the way the mystery of the sacrament of marriage, this 'sacrament of love' as Saint John Chrysostom called it.

So the day would pass without any formality, without anything vaguely resembling formality, in an immense respect for human life and in a sense of joy welling forth in a torrent of life. How could the principal actor not succumb to fatigue? He must have been sustained by some force beyond himself.

There was nothing unusual in what has been described. It was just one Sunday like any other.

4

This is the Church of which I am made a minister to you (Col 1:25)

So that you might be partakers of the divine nature (2 P 1:4)

ALEXANDER MEN CAME into the world at a moment in history when the Christian Church in Russia was being subjected to the most terrible repression by its enemies, intent on its destruction. Such an onslaught on buildings, people, the beliefs of ordinary worshippers, was unprecedented in history, even at the worst moments of the persecutions of Nero and Diocletian. This situation led him to question the mystery of the Church's survival in pagan empires, or in Christian theocracies where compromises with the powers of this world threatened the purity of the Church's message.

He started from the observation that the Roman Empire at the time of Christ was based on solid political and economic foundations. Its borders were secure and a large variety of people coexisted within them. And yet all was not harmonious. Pliny wrote to the emperor: 'These Christians have appeared and our temples are being deserted.' He was in the presence of a mystery beyond the grasp of a mind which had no prior revelation of it. The mystery resided in the fact that the Christian faith was based not on a doctrine or a philosophy, nor indeed on a book, be it the Gospels. It was based on a presence, that of Christ who when two or three were gathered together in his name was there in their midst. A few centuries earlier, the psalmist had sung of the happiness of men gathered together before the face of God who conferred on them his blessing: 'How good and how pleasant it is for brethren to dwell together in unity' (Ps 133:1). It was this tranquil joy of 'togetherness' which set the tone of these early years of Christianity.

Christ left no writings behind, but he left a greater legacy when he said: 'I am with you always, even unto the end of the world' (Mt 28:20). The energy which enabled the Church to withstand the trials and battles of life derived from this togetherness in the presence of the Lord. Its strength was Christ's strength, and the gates of hell which could not prevail against him on Easter Sunday would not prevail against the Church. The deep-seated conviction of the first generation of Christians that the end of the world was imminent diminished with the passing of the centuries. It remained nonetheless true that the world had entered into an eschatological era, which might end tomorrow or in ten thousand years; it would last as long as the Bible's closing supplication: 'Come, Lord Jesus!' had not been fulfilled.

It is impossible to give an adequate definition of the Church. The early Christians made no attempt to codify what was to begin with a lived reality, an experience of life. The word Church comes from the Greek word *Ekklesia*, meaning any sort of political, liturgical or eschatological assembly of persons. This highlights the concept of the Christian faith being lived not in isolation but in togetherness, community. When, in the fourth century, the State under Constantine proposed to come to an agreement with the Church, a number of Christians began to withdraw from a life which had shown itself open to compromise, and they went to live in monasteries or the desert so as to live out fully the gospel message. They did not leave the world in order to condemn it or hurl abuses against it for wallowing in sin; they did so in order to pray for it and enter into its sufferings, and to open up to it new paths of salvation. It was a mystical verification of the monastic adage: 'To be separated from all so as to be united with all.' Father Alexander liked to evoke the luminous figure of Saint Francis of Assisi who went to the very limits of self-abnegation, poverty and asceticism, yet continued to overflow with love for his fellow humans, for animals, for the simplest flower by the wayside. This 'ascetic who loved the world' truly modelled himself on the Gospels.

The Church is not a *sect*—a word deriving from the Latin word meaning 'to cut oneself off' —turned in on itself. It has always sought to be open to the world and receive people into its embrace. It succeeded in establishing a new type of relationship between people, even if it did not always live up to the ideal: 'There is neither Jew nor Greek, there is neither bond nor free, there is neither male nor female; for you are all one in Christ Jesus' (Ga 3:28–29). During the second and third centuries, the Christians gave the impression of living a true community life: 'See how they love each other.'

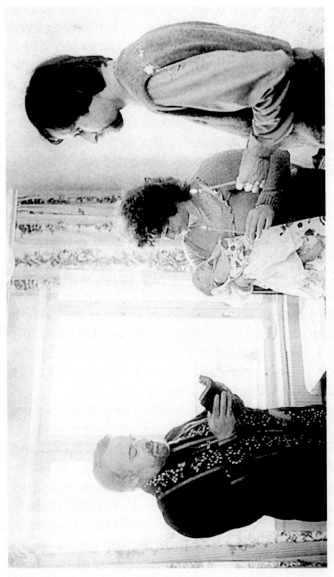

Baptism in an apartment. Photo © Victor Andreev.

This community spirit was perhaps strengthened under the pressure of a largely pagan environment, capable of carrying out bloody repressions when the occasion demanded. It declined with the Middle Ages and drifted dramatically off course, resulting in a whole series of schisms, splits and crises which broke up the unity of the Church. Amongst the persistent attempts to return to the spirit of the primitive community was the foundation of monasticism, where time was divided between prayer, manual or intellectual work, and helping the sick and needy.

Father Alexander continually repeated that Christianity was the religion of man's union with God. The Christian was not simply a consumer of spiritual riches, nor was the Church simply a haven in which to seek refuge; man himself had to take its destiny in hand, for he was responsible for the Church and the treasure it holds. His supreme vocation was to collaborate with God's divine action in the world through love, mutual help, truth, and justice. This vocation made him a 'partaker of the divine nature' (2 P 1:4).

Narrow is the gate which leads to life (Mt 7:14)

The apostolic Church was founded not on the basis of huge buildings adorned with icon screens, in which priests wore sumptuous robes and bells pealed, but on the basis of what created bonds between the members of the community: faith, prayer, mutual help and love.

Later, this same Church presented a picture of desolation, which Alexander Men compared to a flood sweeping along in its waters debris, tree trunks and corpses. Where was the pure water in all this? He recommended a return to the primitive Church of

THE GOSPEL AS CHRIST'S PRESENCE

What explanation can be given for the fact that, in Antiquity, certain groups of Christians were strong enough to attract to themselves the power of the State? You will say that only one word is needed to clarify this: 'The Gospel'. This is true, yet it is not the whole answer. When we refer to the 'Gospel', we immediately think of a book. But the Gospel book was not in a position to conquer the world until a much later date, following the invention of printing. Thus in the nineteenth century, when the Gospel was translated in America, it was awaited so eagerly that it had to be cabled chapter by chapter, from town to town. Nowadays any book can be printed; we live in a civilisation of the book, complicated by video culture. At the time of the early Christians, things were very different; books were few and far between, and though the standard of culture was relatively high, the book played little part in this.

So, when we use the word 'Gospel', we are thinking only of a 'teaching' handed down to us, whereas the key to understanding what happened initially lies in the word *Ecclesia*, meaning 'Church'. The Church triumphed over the State. It was the Church which constituted the Gospel; it was she who won the battle. And if we want to delve deeper, we can say that the victory was due to Christ's mysterious presence in the midst of his people. It was not a question of preaching a specific doctrine, but of an assembly of people truly united by the strength of the divine Spirit.

Alexander Men, *The Church and History*

apostolic times in accordance with the teaching of the Church Fathers, a return which would not simply be an imitation, for that would be impossible given the distance in time. Rather would it be a return to the spirit which motivated the early Christians, making them live on the one hand in communities separate from the world with its corruption and violence, and on the other in permanent openness to the world. The early Christians were acutely concerned with the problems of this world, social, cultural, and even political, and this required of them to play their part in resolving them. Father Alexander followed closely the development of all forms of culture and the way they expressed life. It would upset him when narrow-minded people said to him: the writings of the Church Fathers are what matters, the rest is of no account to salvation! He knew that people who spoke like this had either not read the Church Fathers, or they had not read them in the right way; for their writings expressed a profound interest in all manifestations of art and thought particular to their time.

Believers today had to struggle against the tendency to prize material comfort above all else, to experience religion in only a vague sort of way, and to be drawn into the Church as a place of comfort protecting them from the icy cold outside. But in reacting like this, they had forgotten that God is 'a devouring fire' and that Christ came 'to send fire on the earth' (Lk 12:49). If Christians allowed themselves to be touched, ignited by this fire, they would be able to go where the cold wind was blowing. What was necessary was to rid themselves of the pagan instincts still alive in their soul. But Men did not sink into pessimism. He saw the persistence in the human soul of a high spiritual aspiration, even if it was still tinged with paganism. He referred in this connection to the final conversation of the priest hero, in Graham Greene's novel *The Power and the Glory*, with the lieutenant who led him off to the execution post (priests were forbidden residence in the Mexican province of Chiapas, controlled by Marxists): 'If there are men in your ranks who behave badly, everything collapses, because with you everything depends on men. With us, on the contrary, there may be people who behave badly, but in fact everything is imbued with a life which comes from elsewhere.' The priest is referring here to the divine-human dimension of the Church, which enables it to exist from all eternity and imposes nothing without human collaboration.

The Church's paschal mystery was unendingly repeated. Whenever there were desertions, persecutions, a weakening of faith, there was rebirth, resurrection. The apostles disbanded before the ordeal of their Master's crucifixion, but they came face to face with the risen Lord by the lakeside; in Paul's account, the enemies of Christ raged through the new communities, yet the Christian faith flourished in the way we know. Despite its splendours, the Constantine period let the salt of the Christian message lose its savour by drawing the Church into the heart of this world, but the monastic movement sprung up straightaway as a rejection of worldly comfort. When Christianity was in decline in Byzantium, the 'Slavic takeover' occurred and Russia was baptised among others. To the question: 'Does a period of decadence signal the end of the Church?' there is a ready answer. God always sends prophets to save his people, as in the nineteenth century he sent the Curé d'Ars or Saint Seraphim of Sarov.

This is the Church of which I am made a minister to you

Fr Men's speech at the Olympic Stadium, Easter 1990.
Photo © Alexander Efimov.

Father Men observed with amusement that the house in Paris, where Voltaire had announced that in a hundred years' time the Bible would be found only in antique shops as a reminder of the ignorance of past generations, was the very same place in which the World Bible Society set up its headquarters in the twentieth century! And the Society today was distributing hundreds of thousands of copies of the Bible. In pre-revolutionary Russia, the clergy was in a state of great decadence, priests often reduced to the status of poor functionaries whose children were unable to pursue their studies beyond the seminary. Yet the Revolution did not manage to destroy this lifeless body, and martyrs to the faith were to be counted in their thousands. And now, after the fall of communism, the Church was on its feet again, and people were being baptised in their tens of thousands. It was almost like hearing the voice of the angel saying to the women who had brought the spices to the tomb: 'Why seek ye the living among the dead?' (Lk 24:5).

Father Alexander questioned too the notion of redemption, and in particular the idea of the Church as a place of redemption. He stood vigorously apart from the Western scholastic view of redemption as legal reparation for the offence committed against God by the sinner. To wipe out the offence, it was necessary to appease God's anger by a sacrificial act of redemption. This redemption was obtained by Christ on the cross. But in the view of the Fathers of the Eastern Church, the mystery of redemption concerned man and the whole of nature, which too hoped 'to be delivered from the bondage of corruption into the glorious liberty of the children of God' (Rm 8:21). This mystery embraced a process of purification and transformation of the old man, corrupted by sin, and of his grafting onto the divine life. Through his incarnation, Jesus took upon himself worldly flesh, which was as integral to his nature as the spiritual life. Excepting sin, he lived as a man, eating, drinking, experiencing fatigue or joy, and through him the divine was made immanent in the whole of creation. This notion of redemption was alien to any juridical, legal notion of the substituting of the person of Christ for Adam in order to mitigate the anger of the Father. But with the coming of the Son of God, a healing process was instituted whereby a sick humanity was rescued from sin and death. Christ was not an expiatory victim but a divine therapist, who gave himself voluntarily to death. So, when the day came, as foreseen by the visionary of the Apocalypse, the former heavens would fade away to make way for a new man, risen from the dead, living on a new Earth and under a new Heaven.

5

You renew the face of the earth (Ps 104:30)

Let us walk in newness of life (Rm 6:4)

D URING THE LAST quarter of the twentieth century, Russia was at a turning point in its history; a new era was about to begin. Father Alexander started his work as a priest when Khrushchev's reign was drawing to an end, and he lived through the period of the dismantling and collapse of soviet communism. It was the period when, under Brezhnev, believers were interned in psychiatric asylums; when Andropov, in desperation, tried to return to a politics of austerity; when Gorbachev rowed against the tide of history which was about to sweep him away in order to safeguard what communism had achieved. Even so, the last secretary of the Party deserves great credit for having loosened the screw, thus allowing for greater freedom of speech; it was the period of *glasnost*.

A deep-seated change took place around 1988, on the occasion of ceremonies to mark the millennium of Russia's baptism and to commemorate its saints.

Russians began to think back to their Christian past in the centuries preceding the Revolution, which the Bolsheviks had gone out of their way to conceal. They felt the desire to reconnect with it. The political ideology inspired by Marxism had reached the end of its course; it no longer held the promise of a radiant future and would soon be erased by history.

It has to be admitted, however, that this ideology had left lingering traces on the mentality and behaviour of those who had been subjected to it. Marxism was based on the class struggle as described by Karl Marx in the nineteenth century. It had given rise to a simplistic, somewhat Manichaean way of thinking, which exposed to public contempt 'those who thought differently'. This was how the 'dissidents' who did not conform to the *diktat* of the official line were described. If you do not think like I do and like the party to which I belong, the ideologist stated, you are my adversary and I have to eliminate you. Such an attitude denied any possibility of engagement in dialogue. In official reports, any leaning towards consultation and discussion, any acknowledgement of differing points of view to which the human mind naturally inclines and which are readily accommodated in a climate of tolerance, were nipped in the bud. Such was the impact of totalitarianism.

Dom Helder Camara gave a good definition of tolerance when he said: 'If you don't think like I do, you enrich my way of seeing things.' This freedom of dialogue was still lacking in the political domain in Russia, which had not established any basis of stability. It was still lacking in the Church, many of whose leaders, on the fall of communism, were rushed into posts of responsibility before they had time to work out in their own minds the mystery of life within the Church, which is not to be compared with any human institution. In the case of Father Alexander, whether he was talking to members of the KGB, to Christians of other confessions, to atheists or Buddhists, he could converse easily with all of them, without feeling the least embarrassment; he was open to everybody. This ability to communicate with the most varied people served him in good stead when it came to undergoing the long and painful interrogations which were a more or less regular occurrence in his life.

The Russian Church has gone through its ordeal by fire and martyrdom. In what sort of state has it emerged? Bright gleams of saintliness alternate with zones of darkness. Father Alexander predicted that the fall of atheism, against which the Church had stood united and closed ranks, would unleash divisions and disputes. Paradoxically, he almost dreaded the collapse of the totalitarian system. And indeed the event, when it came, catching unawares the most astute political observers, left the Church reeling.

When freedom came, people reacted in diverse ways. Some, in a great frenzy of activity, started redecorating cupolas and painting frescoes and icons; others let themselves be carried away by the long services and magnificent chanting of the choirs; and overriding everything there was the aura of pathos which hung over the Church establishment itself, with its unctuous language remote from the preoccupations of the modern world and the questionings and searching of the world of culture.

A conservative reaction set in too amidst a noisy minority, nostalgic for the glorious days of the empire and happy to be once again with people like themselves. They sometimes made a great show of their hostility to the foreigner, particularly from the West—communism prohibited contacts with foreigners considered dangerous; they were outwardly hostile towards ecumenism which they considered to be the greatest modern heresy—it is true that the soviet authority used ecumenism to cover up religious persecutions; they were hostile towards any sort of reform: not a single detail was to be changed in Church services, particularly with regard to the use of Slavonic, which most churchgoers, however, no longer understood; it was forgotten, moreover, that the Council of Moscow had met in 1917-1918 to make deep-seated reforms to the Orthodox Church, but had not been able to complete its mission because of the Revolution.

These conservative groups also emitted an odour of racism and anti-Semitism. A large number of Jews had in fact fought with the revolutionaries in 1917, and some of them sympathized with Lenin's hatred of any type of religious expression. It was Kaganovitch who destroyed the Cathedral of the Holy Saviour in Moscow. Father Alexander pointed out, however, that the Russian people themselves, in a rush to destroy everything that was sacred, had given active support to the Bolsheviks in destroying churches, burning icons, and showing their contempt for sacred vessels. Before the Revolution, the situation of Jews was not always enviable because of the anti-Semitism rife in certain Orthodox communities, because too of the restrictions imposed on them with regard, for example, to entry into university or the civil service. Father Alexander had no problem reconciling the fact that he was descended from the people of the Covenant, endowed in his eyes with an exceptional grace, with his sense of belonging to the Russian people whose traditions and culture he so greatly admired, just as he venerated their great figures of saintliness and their religious thinkers who had been such a formative influence on him.

The situation of the patriarch, Alexis II, was a delicate one, for he had to steer a careful course between the many rocks on which his ship might founder. He realized that after decades of persecution, Christians were not yet in a position to respond to the challenges of the modern world: opening up to the West and the movement towards globalization; adapting to new modes of thinking when, officially at least, there had previously been only one, and to new styles of life; accepting new models of family and social life and the impact of the media. The main preoccupation of the Church's leader must clearly be to maintain unity at all costs.

Despite the tensions which on occasions characterized his relationships with other priests or with members of the hierarchy, the priest of Novaya Derevnia never lost hope in the Church—a gathering of sinners journeying towards the Kingdom. However small the number of believers, the Church safeguarded its treasure of sanctity by perpetuating here on earth Christ's incarnation; the Church was His body and He sustained its life. Father Alexander was haunted, however, by the sense of time running out; it was as though he had the presentiment that the end was drawing close. He doubled his efforts, never tiring of addressing the most diverse audiences or communicating in writing with those who were seeking the faith or looking to strengthen it.

For several decades, Father Alexander was bound to a regime of silence outside his own parish, and he was forbidden to speak in public. Then suddenly, and for what were to be the last two years of his life, he was allowed to speak freely once more. He could preach as he liked, address pupils in schools, visit the sick in hospital, participate in lecture programmes on the history of religions, on Russian religious philosophy, on how to become a believer, on the Holy Scriptures, and on the relationship between the Bible and culture. One day a visitor found him buried under a mountain of books. 'Oh! I can see you're very busy.—Busy with what?—I'm taking your time. You've work to do.—You are my work.' The articles he published and the talks he gave on radio and television are too many to be counted.

This new wind of freedom intoxicated him and he lived life at a rapid pace, as though determined to catch up on lost time and not lose a minute of the time that was left. Crowds thronged into clubs and cinema halls to listen to this priest who fascinated them, in his black cassock—or if it was Easter time, a white one—with his pectoral cross clearly displayed. With microphone in hand, he would speak without notes, in a warm voice which put people at their ease. Slips of paper would be passed forward to him with questions on them, to which he would give short, trenchant answers. They would relate to the meaning of life and death, to good and evil, to the relation between eternity and the here-and-now, to the earthly and divine dimensions in the human being. As soon as his face appeared on the television screen, people would telephone their friends to tell them to switch on so as not to miss the message of this extraordinary priest.

Their unbelief shall not cancel God's faithfulness (Rm 3:3)

In Soviet society, atheistic materialism had spread
everywhere; it was the foundation of everything, and
claimed to have answers to the ultimate questions.
Father Alexander debated endlessly with himself on
the meaning of this sudden appearance of atheism in
a country which had adopted the name of 'Holy
Russia'—not that she was holy, but holiness was her
ideal—a country which had been subjected to a vision
of life without God. How was one to explain this total
overthrow of the *Weltanschauung*, as the Germans call
it, of a vision of the world which had endured almost
a millennium? Many historians and thinkers, like
Berdyaev, have been preoccupied by this question.

We have seen that the people themselves had
participated, to a certain extent, in the destruction of
the sacred, as though carried away by a terrible,
all-consuming force. Dostoevsky saw the Russian
people as a 'theophoric people', that is to say, they
were 'bearers of God'. Or rather, they were bearers of
a thirst for transcendence, which was always liable, if
they were not vigilant, to change its orientation. The
political at such moments elevated itself to the meta-
physical, appropriating a power over people's minds
quite alien to the latter, but in keeping with a totalitarian system, which turns people into a 'totality' in the
service of a cause. The first secretary of the French
communist party is remembered for his observation
that 'everything is politics'. A terrible ambiguity then
arises, for in the place of the prohibition to believe in
the divine Word is substituted the obligation to believe
in the party's word. In the last resort man remains
a religious creature, motivated by a belief which
is bound by the restrictions of this world, and thus

FAITH AND MAN

Faith is the pivot upon which man discovers the unity of his own 'self'. For this reason every human being, even a militant atheist, potentially figures as a believer in his own subconscious. There cannot be unbelievers, since the mind of man is made in such a way that he unconsciously strives towards a higher principle than himself. The history of the twentieth century has given us spectacular proof of this. It is useful to be reminded that shortly before his death Mao Zedong confided in a journalist that he had come to an understanding of the mystery of God whilst meditating on the personality cult around himself. He realized that if man was deprived of the representation of God, he would end up divinising anything. This truth struck him with a particular force.

In every country where an attempt has been made to abolish the notion of a divine principle, the latter has immediately been replaced by another principle, considerably more common-place and insignificant. An idol appeared on the scene. In the place of the supreme Meaning of life and of the Creator of the universe were substituted either the mirages of abstract socialism or political figures, the majority of whom were rogues; and so it has always been, in every age.

Alexander Men, *First talk on the Creed of Nicaea-Constantinople* fallible, incapable of assuaging his thirst for the infinite. For it hardly makes sense to rebel against a God who does not exist, yet that is precisely what Lenin did with his anti-God campaign which he waged with such vehemence, for his 'faith' was strong, even if it expressed itself negatively, destructively. The strength of Marxism lay in its messianic role, its unshakeable belief in the coming of paradise, but an earthly one, and the stages towards which could be predicted, right down to the ultimate moment.

The philosophy of the absurd, which led so many to embrace nihilism, attracted Father Alexander's interest, attentive as he was to the major currents of thought of his time. The Sartres or Camus of the world, he wrote, represent the world to themselves as an inhuman place, void of meaning, tragic, for it is a world without God. But when they assert that the world is absurd, without meaning, what these philosophers fail to acknowledge is that such an assertion is only valid by virtue of the representation in man of the opposite, that is, of the notion of meaning. 'The person who has no conception of meaning, can have no feeling for, no comprehension of the absurd.' A fish swimming in water has no idea what water is, for it has no representation of what is dry. One must be convinced of the existence of meaning in order to rebel against the absurd. The one only exists as an antonym of the other. It is less atheism itself which is called into question here, than the reasons for the appearance of atheism. On this question Father Alexander showed himself to be a disciple, amongst others, of Berdyaev, who spoke of 'the worthiness of Christianity and the unworthiness of Christians'. The Church, in the philosopher's view, had cut itself off from the world to concern itself with the idea of individual salvation, thus leaving the field free to atheists in whole areas of life which it should have been the role of the Church, with its compassion and rebellion against injustice, to protect: the poor, the downtrodden, the oppressed. A Christianity deaf to the cries of the unfortunate, indifferent to 'the least' amongst Christ's brethren, led Father Men to speak out against a false form of faith: 'I am sure that not a single church has closed contrary to God's will. Those who were unworthy of it have always been dispossessed of the church. Atheism is the consequence of our own unworthiness. It is not atheism which has to be combated first, but the false Christianity which is to be found in each one of us.'

Atheism thus had a positive role to play. Voltaire's mocking attacks, the Marxist view of religion as 'the opium of the people', Nietzsche's revolt, and even the Russian Revolution, whatever the horrors it perpetrated, had had a purifying effect, raising the spiritual level of Christians and allowing them to appraise these negations of God. Dostoevsky said that his faith had passed through the crucible of doubt, but it was arguable that atheism could go through a similar process. The questions atheists sometimes put to Christians comfortably entrenched in their certainties could strike one as highly pertinent. A Russian theologian and survivor of the Revolution said it would be an excellent idea to establish chairs of atheism in theological institutes, so as to understand the reasons why so many people denied the existence of God in their lives, and to evaluate the part played by Christians in this denial.

Christianity had not put an end to the struggle against the prince of this world, to the struggle between light and darkness. It was still in its infancy and it would be centuries before its word was proclaimed throughout the universe. It was young — 2 000 years old! — in comparison with the thousands of years that paganism had existed. But in the words of Saint John Chrysostom, whom Father Men liked quoting: 'Faith in Christ is eternally renewed.' Many of Christ's words and many of his acts remained incomprehensible to us, 'for we are still Neanderthals as regards our minds and moral understanding, because the arrow of the Gospel is targeted on eternity, because the history of Christianity has only just begun and everything that was done previously, everything we now call the history of Christianity, were only attempts, some of them clumsy, some unfruitful, to realize its goals'.

Despite the divisions he saw within the Russian Church, Father Men remained optimistic. Christianity, in his eyes, was the bearer of a unique message of salvation which would only be realized in times to come. The question of how long the Christian era would last was of little importance. Superstitions, idolatries, the revival of pagan beliefs and practices so popular in our time, underlined how great was the work of purification to be carried out on people's minds. Father Alexander went so far as to say that atheists were sometimes firmer in their convictions than Christians, for they had disciplined themselves throughout their lives to rely only on themselves. The atheists in question were not passive, half-hearted people, but held convictions that had matured over time. There were dedicated Christians who, for their part, would go so far as the sacrifice of their lives when the occasion required, and as an offering to God. But there were those too, who, in times of trial and excessive exposure to suffering, were ready to sever their link with God. The reason why some Christians showed greater weakness than atheists was because they lacked the habit of self-reliance. The Christian was strong only when he felt himself linked to God 'whose strength is made perfect in weakness' (2 Co 12:9).

Christ had promised total power over the world, not through force of arms, nor through fascination with ideologies, nor through economic power, but through love; it was love which it was the Church's role to manifest on earth so as to put an end to tyranny, injustice, corruption, lies. Sanctity was not a stuffy moral attitude; it was a living experience, in communion with One whose power of life triumphed over the work of death. The centrepiece of this life was the chalice, around which Christians were invited to gather in order to draw from it torrents of grace to be poured out onto the world.

We are taken for dying, and behold, we live (2 Co 6:9)

It was in a society which had made atheism its ideal that Father Men wrote his many books on the subject of religion and its influence on the evolution of humanity, even if he was not what might be called a religious historian. The public he was writing for, brought up on materialism, had an essentially scientific way of looking at things and displayed a profound ignorance in matters of religion, which the education system went out of its way to conceal or deliberately distorted. This huge void had to be filled, and as quickly as possible. He quoted statements from the great scientists supporting the idea of the compatibility between science and religion: 'The more involved in science I become, the more of a believer I become' (Pasteur). 'The person who has lost the capacity to wonder and to venerate is no longer alive. To know there exists a hidden Reality which is revealed to us as the supreme Beauty, to know this and to feel it, is at the heart of the authentic religious experience' (Einstein).

The fundamental idea underlying the whole of this historical reflection was that from the Stone Age to the atomic age, religion, whatever form it took, was an integral dimension of the human mind. Christianity itself marked the peak of a long historical process, echoed in the words of Saint Paul: 'When the fullness of time was come, God sent forth his son, made of a woman' (Ga 4:4). Minds had to evolve over a long period before this fullness of time was reached, so that God could arrive on earth as the incarnate Word. That was as far as one could go. People, however, remained free to accept the Good News or to reject it. God forced no-one to enter into his purpose. The ultimate proof of this liberty was the Cross, which Christ willingly embraced. Some desired miracles, others wisdom, but Saint Paul stated: 'We preach Christ crucified, a scandal for the Jews, and folly for the pagans'. There was no other way, Men argued, unless one went back to Buddha, Confucius, Plato, Epicurus.

The establishment of different religions such as Buddhism, Judaism, Islam, and even the Reformation, were important landmarks in the awakening and development of humanity's religious consciousness. Every public campaign against religion—and in Marxist countries it had attained unrivalled proportions— was an admission of the importance religion assumed in people's minds and of its role in the arena of history.

Did the contemporary era, when unbelief was progressing at such a rapid pace, mark the end of religion? Not at all. In Men's view, the very violence of the struggle against it was the guarantee of its vitality. It is worth recalling here that between the Russian Revolution and the Second World War, the number of martyrs to the faith far exceeded those who had died during the first three centuries of Christianity.

Father Alexander was interested in the arguments of atheistic thinkers whom he quoted fairly frequently, as though he was conducting a secret dialogue with them. Nietzsche's assertion that 'God is dead' was accompanied, as he saw it, by a rejection of morality, but also by an inner force of a mystical character embodied in Zarathustra. Camus's desperate atheism was only one side of his nostalgia for God and of his search for a moral support to stop him sinking into the absurd, as is demonstrated by the actions of Dr Rieux in *The Plague*, who throws himself with all his ardour into the fight to save his fellow-men. Even a convinced atheist like Freud asserted that every man firmly believed, if only unconsciously, that he would survive after death. The thought of God never abandoned man. This was demonstrated by the French Encyclopaedists in the middle of the eighteenth century, when they preached the religion of nature or built temples of reason. Sartre wrote that atheists were so obsessed with God's absence that they never stopped thinking about it. In the nineteenth century, the Russian intelligentsia 'went towards the people' in a spirit of selflessness and dedication comparable to that which sent missionaries to preach the word in distant lands. Atheistic humanism of the last three centuries had predicted the demise of religious faith; the Bolsheviks tried to bring about its end by force, yet faith still lived on.

Modern atheism and agnosticism had many causes. Father Alexander listed some of them, starting with the first of all causes: the desire to be 'like gods', the Revolt from before Time. It was a question of recreating the world according to the designs of men, who considered they would have made a better job of it than God did. There were, in this connection, the advances in science, particularly bio-ethics, which encouraged some to delude themselves with the idea that man was becoming a past master of life. Another cause was the urbanisation of large cities, which threatened to submerge the individual in the anonymity of the crowd and destroy his personality, in opposition to religion which, according to one American historian cited by Men, 'remains the most personalized of all forms of human activity'. A finger was pointed too at the spiritual *embourgeoisement* of some sections of society, which had lost touch with the essence of religion and perverted its spirit.[7] Taking all of these factors into account—there were others besides—many were asking themselves: did the Church have a future? To put the question in these terms was to overlook the fact that the Church was not solely a human institution, but a divine-human one, its head being Christ who had said to Peter: 'On this rock I will build my Church and the gates of hell shall not prevail against it' (Mt 16:18). Jesus himself was the builder of the Church. His disciples had to collaborate with him, for if they were silent the stones would cry out.

---

[7] *Embourgeoisement* is the process of migration of individuals into the bourgeoisie, or middle classes, as a result of their own efforts or collective action.

The churches empty? So what? Wasn't it a good deal worse 'when the churches were full and hearts were empty'? The small attendances at church were no proof at all that faith was in decline. Secularisation could not exist alone, for could anyone suppress the tragic dimension of life? Men referred to a survey carried out by a communist historian recording that 90% of the world's population declared themselves believers, even if the figure included a large number of waverers—but the same observation could be made with regard to the atheist ranks.

The twentieth century, then, showed itself to be a religious century, which had produced works of exceptional creativity in every domain: the arts, literature, science, philosophy, and, of course, theology. One of the contemporary world's best-sellers was the Bible, editions of which had attained astronomical figures. Alexander Men was a man of his time. His first studies had been in the scientific field, and he was still passionately attached to biology. 'I would enter a forest or palaeontology museum as though it were a church,' he stated. Close study of the natural sciences gave him the feeling of participating in the divine mystery. This mystery he felt to be encapsulated in two books, the Bible and the book of nature. In this respect he was close to Teilhard de Chardin, whose works he read with great interest. Everything predestined this priest to encounter God here in the world, whatever state the world was in, for as the prayer states, 'the Holy Spirit is everywhere present and fills all things'.

Finally, Christianity could be said to be 'the crisis of all religions'. It was not the revelation of a God consigned for all eternity to heaven; nor was it a philosophical or ethical system; nor was it a form of yoga whereby man gained access into a divine world through asceticism. It was the coming of God-made-Man to earth, to become one with his creature and raise him up to Himself. In the words of the Church Fathers: 'God made himself man so that man could become God.'

Fr Men after questioning. Photo © Sofia Roukova.

There must be divisions amongst you (1 Co 11:19)

Father Alexander devoted a great deal of thought to ecumenism, on the basis of Jesus' prayer: 'May they be one, as you Father are in me and I am in you' (Jn 17:21). He was attentive to the efforts of Christians of every confession to put Jesus' prayer into practice, and did his utmost to keep abreast of initiatives undertaken to this end by different associations and personages throughout the world. He met key people like Cardinal Lustiger, Jean Vanier and Father Daniel-Ange. During the nineteenth century no-one had gone further than Vladimir Soloviev in the field of action and reflection to promote Christian unity, and one can say that Father Men was his counterpart in the twentieth century. His extreme openness was frowned upon, however, by the Russian Church, which still today remains very much closed in on itself and ready to accuse of heresy anything that deviates from its fundamentalist line.

In quoting this paradoxical verse from Saint Paul to the Corinthians—'there must be divisions among you'—Men embarked on a solidly constructed argument on what we might call in Pascalian terms 'the good use of divisions'. He observed that Christianity was one in its essence, its roots, its notion of a divine humanity, its mystical foundation. However, in spirit it was multiform, on the human, cultural or social plane. In contrast to Buddhism or Islam, it had not generated a single form of culture. Its creators were able to construct cathedrals, paint icons, under the pen of Greek and Latin writers develop fertile, far-reaching ideas, elaborate liturgical rituals full of richness and variety; all this diversity was inspired by the unique creative spirit of Christianity.

It was dangerous to present Christianity as being uniform in appearance. Father Men referred in this connection to the Latin-Roman centralism of the Middle Ages: everywhere the same words, the same chants, the same statues, evidence, it was true, of a strong unifying spirit, but to the detriment of the differences which existed between peoples and their cultures. This situation continued up to the Second Vatican Council.

In the second century *Didaché* one reads: 'As this broken bread was scattered over the mountains, and was brought together to become one, so let Your Church be gathered together from the ends of the earth into Your Kingdom.'[8] The separate grains of wheat became one in the unique bread of the Eucharist. During the first millennium of Christianity, diversity and unity were manifested through the action of divine Grace in the creation of different rituals, in the diversity of cultures, and in the way saintliness sprang up in different countries. Unity did not signify uniformity. Each country had to develop its Church life according to its own native traditions. Christianity did not belong to one particular people; its vocation was universal. The first millennium demonstrated that unity and diversity could harmoniously coexist without threatening the integrity of the Church. If Churches became divided, it was precisely from the moment when people could no longer admit that diversity and unity were in every respect compatible. There was no need to fear diversity within the Churches, or to fear the 'other' who was different from ourselves.

Referring to Matthew 16:18, Men asserted that Christ had founded not a variety of Churches but a

8   *Didaché*, 9, 4.

single Church, His own, to be assembled as a single flock under a single shepherd. Church division was the consequence of human sin; in reality, however, 'the Church is one', as Khomiakov had already stated in the nineteenth century; it was 'one' because Christ's body could not be broken into parts, fragmented. Men wrote: 'My conclusion is that the Church is one and that divisions between Christians have come about as a result of political, national, ethno-psychological and cultural differences. They can only be overcome through a spirit of fraternal love.' In the twentieth century, the Churches realized that 'the sins of men are the principal cause of division', and that unity could not be restored by human forces alone. This would come about through ways indicated by Christ. But God was already at work. At the instigation of the abbé Couturier, prayer meetings were being organised in various locations, and people were coming together for worship. Through prayer, a new atmosphere was being created based on mutual understanding, help, and ultimately, love. Overarching these places of prayer—and the monasteries had an important part to play here—an invisible monastery was being built dedicated to prayer and thanksgiving for unity. Many Christians joined this movement, even if they were still in a minority.

It was through the will of the political parties that in 1919, on the occasion of the Treaty of Versailles, the League of Nations was created, with the mission of safeguarding peace and developing international relations. The Churches could not be left behind in this project for world-wide harmony and understanding. Action was undertaken. In 1920, the synod of the Church of Constantinople launched a call for unity.

On the initiative of protestant Churches, a series of
conferences organised in the inter-war years led to the
creation, in 1948, of the World Council of Churches,
which the Russian Orthodox Church became a member of in 1964 at the world assembly in New Delhi,
followed shortly after by the Churches of the satellite
countries. The Catholic Church was not slow to act:
Vatican II's decree on ecumenism transformed relationships between Rome and the other Churches. Men
applauded the meeting between the patriarch Athen-
agoras and Pope Paul VI in 1964, the lifting of anathe-
mas in 1965, and the efforts of John Paul II to drive the
movement forward. The movement was irreversible,
for the vast majority of Churches throughout the world
were behind it.

It is rather strange that Father Men did not go into
the theological issues causing division, nor into the
reasons for the isolationism of the Churches, even
friction between them, which could hardly be left in
the air in any serious dialogue. This was a pity, for he
may have given the impression that unity was already
a reality—for which his detractors criticized him—
without explaining how it had come about. He never-
theless emphasized that unity would not be achieved
through compromise, but through maintaining an
unwavering loyalty to one's own tradition which it
was every believer's duty to deepen.

He referred, in this connection, to the example of
Soloviev, a pioneer of ecumenism, who had returned
from his visit to Europe 'even more orthodox than he
had been before'. For he had seen the West, which up
until then he knew only through books; he had met
people, and he had come to feel in the deepest part of
his soul that in spite of everything he belonged to the

East. His desire to see Church unity become a reality had brought home to him the strength of the tie binding him to his own Eastern tradition. Divisions were necessary, Saint Paul had said. On condition that their human dimensions were taken into account, in the way Soloviev had done.

Contrary to the commandment of love preached by Christ, quarrels and schisms had led to persecutions and religious wars. The Churches were beholden to assume responsibility for world peace and unity. The dissensions referred to were seen as a counter-testimony by those drawn to the Gospel's message of peace and love. The Chinese delegate to the world conference in Edinburgh, in 1910, begged participants not to export divisions born in the West to far away countries in the East, for they were the main obstacle to the development of the Church's mission there. Church unity was a matter not only for specialist theologians. It was the concern of everyone at grass-roots level as they sought to open themselves to other Christians, to seek to know them and understand the values for which they stood, and to experience mutual love. As the Metropolitan bishop Platon of Kiev said: 'The walls between Churches do not rise right up to heaven.'

Father Alexander, it hardly needs stating, had a thorough and intimate experience of atheism. He gravely maintained that, in his view, the struggle Christians had to maintain today was against false Christianity, which adulterated the purity of its message. Atheism was the pernicious fruit of a species of Christian who purported to be the bearer of a message of truth, peace and love, but was unable to put it into practice amongst his fellows. It was easy to denigrate an ideological adversary, but it was hardly the best way to solve the problem of atheism. If Christians were not able to demonstrate, in the face of Marx, that religion was not a form of opium but a generator of life through love, then they were a poor imitation of their Master.

Men's originality lay in the view he expressed that divisions between Christians led not only to an increase in atheism, but to other divisions which were a source of suffering in the world. It is amazing to see how this priest, living his rather reclusive life in his small country church, managed to keep up with, and familiarize himself with the different movements and expressions of Christian faith which came to the fore during his ministry, amongst these the communities of Taizé and L'Arche, the Focolarini, and many others. Christians in the West were drawn by his personality; Cardinal Lustiger said of him: 'He is a man of peace', and Jean Vanier: 'He is a great prophet'. At Novaya Derevnia a small flame flickered in an icy world; unfortunately, it left hidden in the shadows the forces intent on extinguishing it.

6

He shall be saved as by fire (1 Co 3:15)

Watch and pray, for you know neither the day nor the hour (Mt 25:13)

WHEN PEOPLE CAME to see him for the first time Father Alexander would give them a prayer manual, entrusting them to a guide to accompany them on their journey towards God. One day, one such visitor put this question to him: 'Why must one pray with the words of another? God knows I love him, and I like to speak to him using my own words.' The priest replied that it was good to turn spontaneously to God like this, in an intimate relationship with Him, but that it was no less beneficial and necessary to use prayers written by great spiritual thinkers and contemplators of God's beauty, who had a wealth of spiritual experience to draw on. Such prayers were full of inspiration and of God's love, and they revealed a talent and wisdom that a Christian could acquire only gradually.

It was with those Russians in mind who for decades had been cut off from their spiritual roots, and who were drawn to the Church by their thirst for God, that Father Alexander wrote his *Practical Prayer Manual*. It was a sort of guidebook written specifically for people who had very little experience in the domain of spiritual practices; it cleared the terrain and opened up the way for them. Reading such a book can be quite disturbing, for it has the effect, even with believers who think they are well versed in the difficult art of prayer, of calling their practices into question.

People living in the city might have to struggle with acute tensions in the family due to the cramped conditions in which they lived; the same was true of the work place where they were surrounded by all the noise and commotion which is part and parcel of city life. Prayer was first and foremost a gift of grace; it was the divine Spirit entering into one and giving one the desire and strength to enter into a state of prayer. 'Prayer is much more the action of God in us than the outcome of our own personal efforts.'

Prayer also brought physical and mental benefits. In the great ascetic tradition of Eastern Christianity, called *hesychasm*—a word taken from the Greek, meaning peace, serenity—prayer was a search for inner peace, a descending into the depths of the heart to still the agitation there. It was impossible to pray if the heart was agitated or a prey to disorderly passions. A well directed prayer was capable of attenuating most of the problems of daily living: headaches, emotional upsets, psychological traumas, confusion. The body was healthier and sleep sounder; also, Father Alexander maintained, if people today put into practice only half of the precepts of the Sermon on the Mount, their complexes and neuroses would vanish like magic! In liturgical prayers, it was to be recalled, the Master of

Nazareth, who spent a part of his life on earth healing the blind, the crippled, the sick at heart, was referred to as the 'physician of our souls and bodies'. The sacred elements consecrated at the Liturgy were called 'medicine for immortality'. The spirit and the body were indissolubly linked.

It is on the basis of this doctrine that the author gives advice on positions of the body, on concentration, on the rule of prayer, on the struggle against distractions and aridity of the heart. He stresses the importance of withdrawing from the agitation of the world, of learning to master time, and in particular of sharpening the will. 'Let us throw ourselves into the work of prayer,' he stated: the body itself has to actively participate in the process.

The field of prayer was limitless and could embrace every moment of existence. A bird singing, the beauty of a flower, a smile between friends: all of these might fuse into an unceasing song of praise to the Creator. Rote prayers, however, those regular meetings with God in the course of one's daily living, were not to be dispensed with. Father Alexander gave particular emphasis to this point, for they were a crucial means of combating laziness, spiritual sloth, and the dissatisfaction that comes from a Christian life lacking in depth.

Just as before the offertory the believer was beholden to make peace with his neighbour, so before entering into prayer it was necessary to set aside trespasses, avoiding anger and letting oneself be enveloped in silence; only then should one begin to repeat the words, letting them rise up from the heart. Once one had finished praying, it was preferable not to rush straight back into what one was doing but to resume a state of silence, so as to let the words germinate in one's soul.

PERPETUAL PRAYER

The Fathers claimed that perpetual prayer is the goal towards which every person of piety should aspire. This may seem strange. What would one say of a person who prays continuously? That he's a lunatic, sick, a fanatic? In fact, perpetual prayer is something quite normal; it is the aim of the Christian life. This does not mean that the believer should spend his entire day reciting prayers; it means that he spends his life face to face with God: whether he is laughing or crying, tired or refreshed, sad or joyful, he is always conscious of God's presence. He can thus continually orientate his life in relation to God, in thankfulness, prayer, repentance: You are here, beside me. Such a way of being permeates the soul and makes it more lucid. But to reach that point, you have to start with the rules of prayer.

We are referring here to the higher reaches of prayer. The first rungs on the ladder are morning and evening prayers, which should be read assiduously with the help of the *Book of Prayers*; or they should be learned by heart one after the other. To know them thoroughly is of the utmost importance, for then they penetrate to the depths of the soul and are a powerful aid against the forces of darkness surrounding us.

There you are experiencing fear, anxiety, distress, or you are in an execrable mood; you start repeating the sacred words, and bit by bit, like Orpheus with his power to calm wild animals, the words restore order to your soul.

Alexander Men, *Practical Prayer Manual*

Most important of all, one should not think that because one had prayed, one was even with God.

In this book of initiation to prayer, perpetual prayer, the highest stage of all and reached by only a very few, is also analysed. The Bible sometimes evokes a spiritual state beyond what we think of as conscious activity, in which prayer comes about of itself, even during the night-time: 'I sleep, but my heart is awake' (Sg 5:2); Paul himself invites us to 'pray without ceasing' (1 Th 5:17). This type of prayer is very demanding; it requires great powers of concentration and, in particular, a special grace. It differs fundamentally from the type of meditation practised in the Far East, called *mantra*, for it does not aim at the spirit's immersion in some sort of spiritual abyss or undifferentiated whole. Every Christian prayer is an encounter with someone, who is both in the world and above the world. Perpetual prayer can become dangerous if it is not accompanied by humility and repentance.

'Lord Jesus-Christ, son of God, have mercy on me a sinner.' This is what is called the Jesus Prayer, for the name of Jesus is at its core and illuminates it from within. It is also called the prayer of the heart for it must be absorbed into the heart, into one's unconscious depths. This is why the supplication: 'Lord have mercy' (*Kyrie eleison*) is sometimes repeated a great many times. Only a small number of these repetitions attain consciousness; most of them fall into the unconscious, into the depths of the 'self' beyond the reach of external forces; it is they which need to be stirred into being, for in them is located the source of sin and the source of good.

This prayer is addressed to the God of the Trinity: we associate ourselves with Christ's prayer in his relation to the Father, and through the force of the Spirit which makes us say that Jesus is Lord, we accede to the heart of the Father as his children.

This prayer brings us into communion with others, whom we pray for wherever we meet them, in the street, the metro, when shopping. Sometimes it may seem to us that we are surrounded by disagreeable, uneducated people who push aside everyone in their path; but the prayer acts as a protection, allowing us to construct what Saint-Exupéry calls 'the inner citadel'.

This Jesus prayer is the creative Word through which everything was made; it is of cosmic origin too. It can embrace the whole of creation, fields, plants, birds, mountains, oceans, all of nature. It strengthens the impulse carrying all of these things towards God.

Father Alexander advised that prayer should be reinforced by the liturgical and sacramental life, of which it was the extension in daily life. At Novaya Derevnia, the liturgical offices were simple and of great beauty. A large number of the pastor's sermons have been recorded. They are relatively short and are presented very clearly, so as to be accessible to everyone; yet their depth is apparent at the same time, whether in the explanation of a liturgical event, the exposition of the life of a saint, or advice regarding the way the obstacles we encounter on our spiritual path through life may be overcome. Father Men had a gift with words which enabled him to touch the hearts of his listeners. His vast memory allowed him to feel at ease with the most diverse subjects. Obedient to his Church's tradition, he celebrated the Liturgy in Slavonic, whilst fully aware that one day the great riches of what is called the Byzantine ritual would have to be transposed into a language more accessible to today's world. He was especially keen to encourage the active participation of the faithful in the Liturgy, rather than to see them as passive bystanders. He desired them to attend church as often as possible, but without drawing too much attention to themselves, and to participate in frequent communion.

Father Alexander's reflections on prayer were enriched by his reading of the Bible, which occupied an important place in his life as a priest. In a book entitled *The Bible and Literature,* he studied the reflection of the scriptures in Russian and foreign literatures from antiquity up to the twentieth century. In a more or less conscious manner, the Bible had been a continuous source of artistic inspiration through the centuries. The faithful were encouraged to read it on their own or in groups, to consult commentaries so as to deepen their understanding of it, and to compare different translations so as to approach the text with greater refinement. Read in a spirit of sanctity, the Bible was a true 'prayer manual'. Prayer ran through it from beginning to end, starting with Abraham's intercession on behalf of a scattering of righteous who would save Sodom, and culminating in the host of the righteous in the Apocalypse who worshiped in adoration the marriage of the Lamb and awaited his ultimate return: 'Come, Lord Jesus!'

The Soviet regime sought to ban prayer, as well as the Bible which ceased to be published. They were designated as illusory activities which distracted people from the problems of reality. But the need to pray, to enter into union with the mysterious force which was the origin of life and held each person's destiny in its hands, was an inherent part of the human condition. Father Alexander recounted the story of the atheist who had led a pleasurable existence and known happiness, but then, as his life was drawing to a close, felt a touch of sadness, for he didn't know to whom he should say thank you. The priest saw this as a call to express his gratitude to God.

Enter into the joy of your Lord (Mt 25:23)

On Sunday 9 September 1990, Father Alexander set off to church along the footpath bordered by trees and hedgerows. The sun had risen on a cool, clear morning, and there was not a soul to be seen. The assault came from behind; the axe struck down on him, and he struggled back to his house where he collapsed in a pool of blood.

The news quickly spread to those he had nurtured in the faith. They were numb with horror. How was it possible? Father Zielinski wrote: 'I am sure that if his murderer had spoken to him for a minute or two before striking the blow, he would have had a change of heart. But he struck from behind, and no word was spoken.'

Father Alexander remained a priest right through to the end. Aged fifty-five, he had been in the priesthood for thirty-three years, the age of Christ. He was on his way to celebrate the great mystery of the bloodless sacrifice, in the image of Christ to whom he had given his life. He did not realize that on this particular day he would be making the offering, not of bread and of wine, but of his own body. His days were numbered, as he was aware, and he carried out his many activities with a sense of urgency. A new era was about to dawn; it was important to be ready for it.

_ *He shall be saved as by fire*

Funeral of Fr Alexander at Novaïa Dérévnia, 11 September 1990. Photo © D. R.

33

A sort of presentiment concerning the last end—but who in Russia during the last two centuries had not felt that a tragic break in history was about to occur and that 'the time was at hand'?—had led him to meditate on the Apocalypse and to write a sustained commentary on it. This book followed the deep processes of his own spiritual thought, the denunciation of the work of the Beast which came up from the earth, of modern Babylon given over to the powers of this world and to Satan, but also on the revelation of the heavenly Liturgy around the slain and resurrected Lamb triumphing over the work of death. One of the elders says to the visionary of Patmos: 'Those arrayed in white robes are are the ones who come out of the great tribulation ... The Lamb will shepherd them and lead them to living fountains of waters. And God will wipe away every tear from their eyes' (Rev 7:14,17).

There remains the mystery of his death, the horror of such a vile act committed at a moment in history when Russia was rediscovering its spiritual freedom, with regard to which Father Alexander remained so apprehensive. How could one begin to comprehend what God intended by his death? In the eyes of some, the struggle for Russia and its people had started, and the first to fall would be those at the forefront of the struggle. Given his family forebears, it was considered that those behind the assassination were violent anti-Semites.

Others were more ready to attribute it to the work of the KGB, the state police, some of whose leaders were astonished, even bewildered when, after decades of their relentless struggle to eradicate the nation's religious roots, they saw in front of them on television, on the radio, on public platforms, a man freely preaching the Christian teaching which Marx had described as the opium of the people. Such a dramatic, unexpected turnabout threw people into complete disarray. An investigation was undertaken, but it failed to shed any light on the person or persons responsible for the crime, which immediately calls to mind the case of another priest and dedicated servant of Christ, Father Jerzy Popiełuszko of Poland. Two men crushed by the cold monster of the State. Two men struck down by the bitter adversaries of the One who said: 'I am meek and humble of heart.'

What is the situation now? Those he nurtured in the faith have been orphaned of their priest, but his voice is still heard to save them from despair. A pastor has moved on, and the gap left by his departure is waiting to be filled by new vocations still in the making. Above all is the need to escape the temptation of vengeance. 'If someone offends you, Father Alexander said, think not of the one who has committed the offence but of Jesus Christ; drive out the thought of the offence as soon as it appears; turn your attention instead to the clouds and the stars, seek to be calm by rising above the situation, judge it from on high, from afar, as though you were dead and surveying your life from another world… Avoid conflict.'

Metropolitan Anthony (of Sourozh) quotes the words of a man of great spirituality speaking to someone who was in a state of deep despair: 'Do not waste yourself in grief. The Church is a cohort of soldiers that nothing will destroy: every soldier who has fallen on the battlefield rises up for eternity as a suppliant, a protector, an indomitable warrior for the immortal army of Christ. Offer your soul to Christ and His Truth, give your life for the salvation of your neighbour, and you will take your place amongst the immortal combatants of Christ.'

Lightning Source UK Ltd.
Milton Keynes UK
UKOW050017081211

183383UK00001B/5/P